Insects and Spiders

of the World

VOLUME 3
CARRION BEETLE – EARWIG

Marshall Cavendish
New York • London • Toronto • Sydney

Marshall Cavendish
99 White Plains Road
Tarrytown, New York 10591

Website: www.marshallcavendish.com

Library of Congress Cataloging-in-Publication Data
Insects and spiders of the world.
    p.   cm.
    Contents: v. 1. Africanized bee–Bee fly — v. 2. Beetle–Carpet beetle — v. 3. Carrion beetle–Earwig — v. 4. Endangered species–Gyspy moth v. 5. Harvester ant–Leaf-cutting ant — v. 6. Locomotion–Orb-web spider — v. 7. Owlet moth–Scorpion — v. 8. Scorpion fly–Stinkbug — v. 9. Stone fly–Velvet worm — v. 10. Wandering spider–Zorapteran — v. 11. Index.
    ISBN 0-7614-7334-3 (set) — ISBN 0-7614-7335-1 (v. 1) — ISBN 0-7614-7336-X (v. 2) — ISBN 0-7614-7337-8 (v. 3) — ISBN 0-7614-7338-6 (v. 4) — ISBN 0-7614-7339-4 (v. 5) — ISBN 0-7614-7340-8 (v. 6) — ISBN 0-7614-7341-6 (v. 7) — ISBN 0-7614-7342-4 (v. 8) — ISBN 0-7614-7343-2 (v. 9) — ISBN 0-7614-7344-0 (v. 10) — ISBN 0-7614-7345-9 (v. 11)
    1. Insects. 2. Spiders.   I. Marshall Cavendish Corporation.

QL463 .I732 2003
595.7—dc21

                                        2001028882

ISBN 0-7614-7334-3 (set)
ISBN 0-7614-7337-8 (volume 3)

Printed in Hong Kong

06 05 04 03 02   6 5 4 3 2 1

Brown Partworks Limited
Project Editor: Tom Jackson
Subeditor: Jim Martin
Managing Editor: Bridget Giles
Design: Graham Curd for WDA
Picture Researcher: Helen Simm
Illustrations: Wildlife Art Limited
Graphics: Darren Awuah, Dax Fullbrook, Mark Walker
Indexer: Kay Ollerenshaw

Marshall Cavendish
Editor: Joyce Tavolacci
Editorial Director: Paul Bernabeo

WRITERS

Dr. Robert S. Anderson
Richard Beatty
Dr. Stuart Church
Dr. Douglas C. Currie
Trevor Day
Dr. Arthur V. Evans
Amanda J. Harman
Dr. Rob Houston
Anne K. Jamieson

Becca Law
Professor Steve Marshall
Jamie McDonald
Ben Morgan
Dr. Kieren Pitts
Rebecca Saunders
Dr. Joseph L. Thorley
Dr. Gavin Wilson

COVER: Weevil **(NHPA)**
TITLE PAGE: Rhinoceros beetle **(Artville)**

PICTURE CREDITS
Agricultural Research Service, USDA: 157b, Scott Bauer 153, 171t, Keith Weller 159t; **Ardea**: J. L. Mason 156, Pascal Goetgheluck 188; **Art Explosion**: 157t, 159b, 171b, 173t, 183t, 183b; **Artville**: Burke & Triolo 177t; **Bruce Coleman Collection**: J. Brackenbury 160, Jane Burton 154, John Cancalosi 138, M. P. L. Fogden 170, 172, Sir Jeremy Grayson 165, Dr. M. P. Kahl 184, Steven C. Kaufman 161, Hans Reinhard 155b, Jens Rydell 150, Kim Taylor 134, 148, 151; **Educational Images Ltd**: Ron West 139, 164, 177b; **Dr. A. V. Evans**: 133, 137, 141t, 143, 144, 152, 163; **Image Ideas Inc**: 173b; **Steve Marshall**: 175; **NHPA**: ANT/Otto Rogge 147, N. A. Callow 162, James Carmichael Jr. 140, 141b, 178, Stephen Dalton 187, Hellio & Van Ingen 180, Martin Harvey 136t, Daniel Heuchlin 155t, Steve Robinson, Robert Thompson 182; **Oxford Scientific Films**: G. I. Bernard 169, J. A. L. Cooke 166, D. G. Fox 145, Tim Shepherd 189; **Science Photo Library**: Ken Eward 176

CONTENTS

CARRION BEETLE

As their name suggests, carrion beetles feed on the flesh of dead animals. Some species that bury the bodies of dead animals are called "undertaker beetles."

The carrion beetles are brightly colored and relatively large beetles, up to 1.5 inches (38 mm) long. They are usually found on the carcasses of dead animals. Some carrion beetles work together to bury the bodies of animals such as mice and shrews and are called undertaker, sexton, or burying beetles.

There are about 200 species of carrion beetles in the world, with 30 species in North America. Unlike many other insect groups, most species occur in cooler regions. Only a few live in the warmer tropics. Most of these beetles feed on carrion (the flesh of dead animals) as adults and larvae, but a few eat snails or caterpillars. Some even feed on living plants and can be agricultural pests. Carrion beetles occasionally eat other insects such as fly larvae, and they can be found on dung or rotting plants.

Feeding on large animals

There are two main groups of carrion beetles. One group lays eggs near the carcasses of large animals such as foxes,

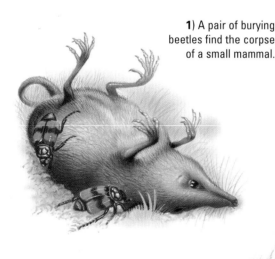

1) A pair of burying beetles find the corpse of a small mammal.

2) The beetles bury the carcass, then strip the fur and shape the flesh into a ball before laying eggs in a chamber nearby.

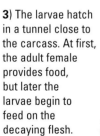

3) The larvae hatch in a tunnel close to the carcass. At first, the adult female provides food, but later the larvae begin to feed on the decaying flesh.

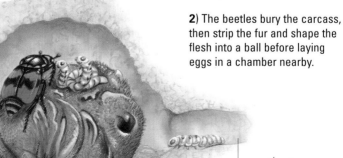

▲ *How burying beetles provide food for their young.*

egg chamber

deer, and raccoons, often after the animal has been dead for a week or more. The larvae crawl onto the rotting carcass and feed on the carrion before pupating in the soil.

Burying the dead

The other group includes the burying beetles. A male and a female of these large red or orange and black beetles find the body of a small animal (usually a mouse, shrew, small bird, or even a snake) and, working together, dig a shallow hole under the carcass until it sinks underground. They then strip the carcass of fur or hair and shape what remains into a ball. The male then leaves, while the female lays up to 30 eggs in a tunnel she digs in the soil.

When the larvae hatch, they move onto the rotting carcass and group together in a hole made by the mother. The mother then feeds the larvae with a liquid consisting of partially digested food from her stomach. After a few hours, the larvae begin to feed on the carrion. The female stays with the larvae and protects them from intruders. She only leaves when, after around 10 days, the larvae begin to pupate. Burying beetles are one of only very few beetles that care for their young.

Symbiotic mites

Burying beetles can only bury small carcasses—anything larger would take too long. They go to the trouble of burying the carcasses to prevent them from being overrun by flies. However, that is not all they do to protect the food of their larvae. Burying beetles also carry a number of different species of mites. When the beetles find a carcass, the mites leave them to feed on fly eggs and larvae. The mites were thought to be parasites but are now known to have a symbiotic relationship with the beetles from which both animals benefit. The beetles act as vehicles, carrying the mites to new food sources, and in return the mites stop the carcass from becoming infested with fly larvae.

Rare and declining beetles

Recent studies have shown that *Nicrophorus pustulatus*, a rare North American species, seems to be associated with carrion in snake dens, where they feed on dead snakes and eggs. The largest North American species, the American burying beetle, was once common but now, for unknown reasons, is very rare. Great efforts are being made to save it from extinction.

Despite their feeding habits, carrion beetles are not known to carry any diseases. They reduce fly numbers and help in the recycling of dead animals.

▲ *This type of carrion beetle does not feed on meat, but it is still found around carrion, feeding on maggots that are developing inside the carcass.*

DISTRIBUTION

AMERICAN BURYING BEETLE, RANGE 1940

AMERICAN BURYING BEETLE, RANGE TODAY

SEE ALSO

- Beetle
- Dung beetle
- Ground beetle
- Scarab beetle
- Symbiosis
- Tick and mite

CENTIPEDE

These long, flattened animals are named for their many legs. Centipedes are fierce predators, injecting poison into prey using fangs that evolved from the first pair of legs.

Centipedes are just one part of a large group of arthropods called the myriapods, which also includes millipedes and some less well-known animals, the Symphyla and Pauropoda. The term *myriapod* means "many-legged," and all adult members of the group have at least nine pairs of legs as well as a pair of antennae.

Centipedes have segmented antennae, which are used to detect movement and smells. Most centipedes are dark orange or brown, though some also have green stripes. Although they are related to insects, centipedes and other myriapods differ in many ways. They lack wings, and the body is not divided into thorax and abdomen. It is, however, divided into many segments, each of which bears a pair of legs.

Like insects, centipedes take in oxygen from the air through a series of tubes that extend into the body. Insects can close off these tubes in dry conditions, but centipedes are unable to do this. Therefore, they usually live in damp and humid environments, where the risk of drying out is small.

There are four types of centipedes, which between them include about 3,000 species. Although they are found around the world, they are most common in the warm tropics, where they can get all the heat and moisture they need.

Most species are less than 2 inches (5 cm) long. However, the world's largest centipede, *Scolopendra gigantea* from South America, can be up to 12 inches (30 cm) long. While most centipedes are completely harmless to humans, a bite from a giant centipede causes fever, vomiting, and intense pain. Very rarely, a bite from a giant centipede can kill someone.

The centipede body

Some centipedes have compound eyes similar to insects, but most centipede eyes are far simpler, and many species have none at all. Sight is not very important to the centipedes, as the majority are nocturnal and come out to

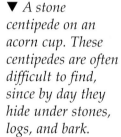

▶ *The internal anatomy of a male centipede. The malphigian tubule is part of the excretory system, while the testis produces sperm.*

▼ *A stone centipede on an acorn cup. These centipedes are often difficult to find, since by day they hide under stones, logs, and bark.*

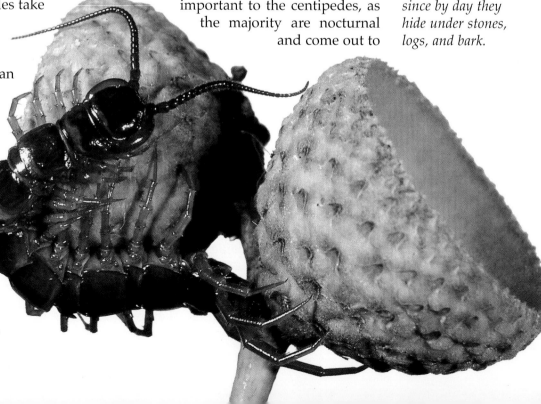

ANATOMY OF A CENTIPEDE

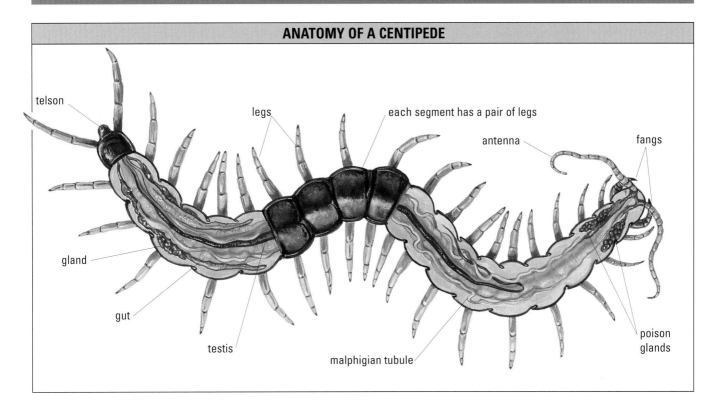

telson

legs

each segment has a pair of legs

antenna

fangs

gland

gut

testis

malphigian tubule

poison glands

hunt at night. In the day, centipedes often hide away under stones, logs, and leaf litter. Some species have a disk-shaped organ at the base of each antenna that is sensitive to sound. Centipedes have three sets of mouth-parts: a pair of biting jaws, a fused lower lip, and a pair of longer mouthparts that are used to handle food.

The number of legs varies according to the species, ranging from 15 to almost 180 pairs. The first pair of legs behind the head have evolved into fangs. These each have a small hole at the tip, through which the animal injects neuro-toxins into its prey. Neurotoxins are poisons that act swiftly on the nervous system, paralyzing the prey completely. Centipedes also have a flattened body that allows them to move freely through their habitat in search of prey.

Centipedes are predators, feeding on insects, other small arthropods, slugs, and earthworms. Some of the largest centipedes can even tackle small mam-mals, frogs, lizards, or birds. They rely on speed to catch their prey. Centipedes will also scavenge for food and feed on dead or dying animals.

Centipede defenses

Centipedes themselves are often eaten by larger predators, such as birds and mammals. There are even some snakes that feed almost exclusively on centipedes. A few centipedes, however, have a neat trick to fool predators—some of their body segments can drop off, with the legs still wiggling. The legs may even rub together to make a noise. This distracts the predator, allowing the centipede to make a quick exit.

Many centipedes have sharp spines on their legs to deter predators. Some also release chemicals that can be smelly or irritating, or they may be sticky. Sticky chemicals slow down fast-moving predators such as ants.

Running without tripping

Centipedes run by carefully coordinat-ing the movement of their legs, so it appears that a wave of motion passes along the body. The legs stretch out sideways, helping the centipede to maintain stability as it runs. In most species of centipedes the length of the legs increases along the body. When the centipede runs in pursuit of an insect,

KEY FACTS

Name
Giant centipede (*Scolopendra gigantea*)

Distinctive features
Up to 12 inches (30 cm) long; largest of the centipedes

Breeding
Eggs laid in damp soil, in clusters of up to 120 eggs; female tends the eggs and young

Food
Large inverte-brates, small mammals, frogs, and reptiles

Distribution
Tropical areas of South America

▲ *House centipedes commonly prey on household pests. This one is feeding on a cockroach.*

evolved, so potential mates do not confuse each other with prey. Mating centipedes circle each other, each tapping its partner with its antennae. The male deposits a small parcel of sperm on the ground, or sometimes in a silken web, and the female picks it up. Some species of centipedes, however, do not carry out courtship. The male simply leaves the sperm package on the ground for a passing female to find.

Guarding the eggs
After the sperm have fertilized the eggs, females of some species lay single eggs into holes in the soil, often coating them with a liquid that kills fungal spores. They then cover the eggs with soil before abandoning them. However, some female centipedes dig a small chamber in the earth, usually under a stone. Into this chamber the female lays a small cluster of eggs. The centipede wraps herself tightly around the eggs and occasionally licks them to remove fungal spores. If an egg is dislodged from the main cluster,

the longer legs behind step up and over the shorter ones in front, preventing the centipede from tripping.

Courtship
In predatory animals with poison-filled fangs, it is not surprising that courtship rituals have

▶ *Giant* Scolopendra *centipedes are able to feed on small verte-brates such as lizards and mice.*

the female gently replaces the egg in the nest. If other insects such as ants threaten the eggs, she will attack them fiercely and attempt to drive them off.

Sharing our homes

The house centipede (*Scutigera coleoptrata*) has very long, thin legs. The ones farthest from the head are longest and can step over the shorter ones when the animal is traveling quickly—these centipedes can run at more than 1 foot (33 cm) per second. House centipedes are commonly found throughout the eastern United States and Canada, and although they often live beneath log piles, stones, and bark, they also wander into people's houses. At night, they emerge from their hiding places and hunt for food; spiders and insects are their favored prey. House centipedes are completely harmless to humans. They may be useful since they feed on undesirable insects such as cockroaches.

Growing up

In species that lay clusters of eggs, the young centipedes look very much like miniature adults, with the same number of legs and segments as the mature form. The female continues to guard the young after hatching, only leaving after they have molted several times and are able to hunt for themselves. This level of parental care is very unusual; after laying their eggs, most arthropods leave their young to survive alone.

The young of species that lay single eggs are born with just seven pairs of legs. At each molt, the young centipedes acquire an extra segment and an extra pair of legs. The length of time and number of molts that centipedes go through before reaching maturity varies greatly. Some take as long as four years to reach adulthood, while others are fully grown in only a couple of months.

SEE ALSO

- *Arthropod*
- *Feeding*
- *Locomotion*
- *Millipede*

CICADA AND HOPPER

Cicadas and hoppers are insects that use piercing mouthparts to suck sap from plants. The mating calls of many cicadas are among the noisiest of any animal.

Cicadas and hoppers belong to a large group of insects known as the bugs. Unlike other bugs, cicadas and hoppers cannot fold away their mouthparts under the body, and their wings form a sloping tent shape rather than folding flat when they are closed.

Cicada characteristics
Adult cicadas are generally bigger than hoppers. Most cicadas are 0.4 inches (1 cm) long, although one common Malaysian species has a wingspan of up to 8 inches (20 cm). Cicadas are typically dull brown or green. Unlike hoppers, most cicadas have a simple body shape. They also have long, see-through wings, prominent compound eyes, and a broad, blunt head. They are most common in warm or tropical countries, but they also live in cooler, temperate parts of the world.

The song of the cicada
Cicadas and hoppers both use sound to attract their mates. The mating calls of hoppers are transmitted as vibrations through plants, but they are too quiet to be heard by the human ear. By contrast, male cicadas produce the loudest sounds of any insect. Some tropical cicadas can be heard from up to 1 mile (1.6 km) away, and the chorus produced by males singing together can fill the air with a deafening drone.

An adult male cicada produces his song by clicking two drumlike membranes, called tymbals, on either side of the abdomen. Muscles inside the abdomen pull the tymbals inward,

causing them to buckle and click like a tin lid. The tymbals click in and out hundreds of times a second, producing a very loud and high-pitched noise. Each species of cicada has a distinctive song to attract females of the same species. To our eyes, cicadas often look

▲ *The pointed body shape of these treehoppers on a branch in Costa Rica fools predators into thinking they are thorns.*

very similar, and some species can only be told apart by comparing their songs. Males usually perch motionless in trees while singing, but they sometimes go for brief flights between songs. When females are nearby, the males switch from their calling songs to courtship songs to encourage the females to mate.

The cicada life cycle

Most of a cicada's life is spent underground, where the wingless young insect, called a nymph, feeds on the watery sap of plant roots. Cicada nymphs have large, shovel-like front legs for digging. The nymphs can live underground for several years or more. When they are large enough to molt into adults, the nymphs dig their way out of the ground, climb up a tree trunk, and shed their skin for the final time.

Among the best-known cicadas are the periodical cicadas of the United States. All the nymphs in a certain area emerge from the ground at the same time. Amazingly, these mass emergences only happen every 13 or 17 years. Some cicadas emerge after 13 years of development, while others wait for a further 4 years. However, the resting period sometimes switches between the two. The emergence takes place over several days in early summer. It can be a spectacular sight—a single tree may be covered with many thousands of empty cases left by the molting cicada nymphs. Even more impressive is the deafening chorus that follows. The sound of millions of cicadas singing together travels for many miles. Adult periodical cicadas live for about a month—just enough time to mate and lay eggs.

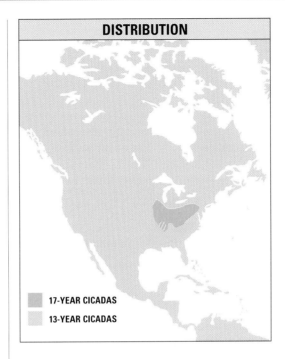

DISTRIBUTION

17-YEAR CICADAS
13-YEAR CICADAS

KEY FACTS

Name
Periodical cicadas (*Magicicada* species)

Distinctive Features
Black body, red eyes and wing veins; male has loud mating call

Habitat
Woodland; female lays eggs in roots of oak, hickory, and other trees

Breeding
Female cuts holes in twigs and lays about 20 eggs inside

Food
Nymph sucks sap from roots; adult feeds on the juices inside twigs

◀ *It is very unusual to see a cicada nymph like this one above ground. Their wingless bodies are better suited for life under the soil, where they feed on plant juices with their pointed mouthparts.*

Irregular life cycle

Periodical cicadas are very unusual because they have an irregular life cycle. Most insects reproduce at regular intervals, such as once a year. However, young periodical cicada nymphs spend many years underground feeding on sap from plant roots.

The adults from some species emerge every 13 years, while other species emerge every 17 years. However, scientists have discovered that the nymphs of any of these species can slow or speed up the development by four years and so emerge after 13 or 17 years. Amazingly, many thousands of cicadas will still emerge within seven days of each other, even when the life cycle has changed in length.

Scientists think switching between a 13-year and 17-year life cycle keeps the cicadas safe from predators. This is because the changing length of the life cycle makes it impossible for a predator to predict in which year the next emergence will occur.

A variety of hoppers

Hoppers are relatives of cicadas that are better known for their jumping abilities than their songs. Many species have very powerful hind legs that enable them to leap away from danger in a split second. There are four main types of hoppers: planthoppers, froghoppers, treehoppers, and leafhoppers. Unlike the cicadas, many species of hoppers have evolved elaborate body forms that disguise the insects, helping them avoid being seen by predators.

Planthoppers are mostly small, sap-sucking insects up to 0.2 inches (5 mm) long. Many feed on plants of the grass family, including crops such as rice,

▼ *An adult 17-year periodic cicada from the Midwest. Scientists think that developing nymphs can count the years by sensing the seasonal growth changes in the trees on which they feed.*

corn, and sugarcane. The Asian brown rice planthopper is one of the most serious crop pests in Asia. Not only does it damage plants as it feeds on their sap, but it also spreads deadly viruses from plant to plant.

Big bugs

The largest planthoppers are the lantern bugs, the biggest of which can grow up to 4 inches (10 cm) in length, with wingspans of 6 inches (15 cm). Lantern bugs are found only in tropical or subtropical countries.

Many are spectacularly colored, with delicate wings that sometimes sport striking eyespots. Lantern bugs have bizarrely elongated heads that are often adorned with bright colors, patterns, or projections. One Brazilian species of lantern bug has a head like a crocodile's. The name lantern bug comes from early, incorrect reports that the heads of these bugs glow in the dark.

Froglike insects

Froghoppers are so-called because their squat shape and powerful leaps make these bugs look like miniature frogs. Some froghopper nymphs are known as spittlebugs because they live inside a mass of frothy bubbles, sometimes called cuckoo spit,

SEE ALSO
- *Assassin bug*
- *Bug*
- *Insect life cycle*
- *Leaf bug*
- *Metamorphosis*
- *Water bug*

◄ *An adult dogday cicada emerges from the skin of its wingless nymphal form. The insect's wings take a few minutes to harden before it can fly away.*

for protection. A froghopper nymph makes its bubble nest by blowing air through watery droppings as it passes out of the anus (rear gut opening).

Not just trees

Treehoppers are tiny bugs that, despite the name, feed on all types of plants. Adult treehoppers often have large, backward-pointing spines extending from their backs, and this has earned treehoppers the nickname "thorn bugs." In some species, the spine provides superb camouflage, making the bugs look like thorns. Other species have oddly shaped spines that make them difficult to swallow, and some have highly complex spines that make the bugs look like ants. The nymphs of many treehoppers produce a sugary substance called honeydew, on which some ants feed. In return, the ants protect the nymphs from predators.

Largest family

Leafhoppers are found throughout the world and make up the largest family of hoppers, with at least 20,000 species.

Scientists think that nearly every plant species on Earth is fed on by at least one leafhopper species. Most leafhoppers suck on sap, but a few species suck out the liquid from individual plant cells. Many are pests of crops. The green rice leafhopper once infested rice fields in such numbers that piles of the insects could be swept up and sold as bird food.

▼ *The green wings of this planthopper from the southern United States have veins that make the wings look remarkably like small leaves.*

CLICK BEETLE

Click beetles have a unique way of righting themselves if they fall on their backs. By flexing the joint between the first two segments of the thorax, they can launch themselves into the air.

Click beetles are common beetles, varying in size between 0.05 and 2.5 inches (1 and 63 mm) long. Many species are nocturnal (active at night) and hide away during the day under rocks, in dead vegetation, or under bark. Some species are commonly found around lights at night or on vegetation. Others can be found during the day on vegetation or flowers, flying along forest edges and trails, and through clearings in woodland. Nearly all click beetles are good fliers.

Worldwide there are almost 10,000 species of click beetle. Most species are found in warm tropical regions close to the equator, but almost 1,000 species are known to live in parts of Canada and the United States.

What's clicking?

Click beetles are recognized by their distinctive elongated form and by the unusual backward-pointing corners at the rear of the pronotum, a shield extending from the thorax (midbody) over the head. When one of these beetles falls on its back or is turned over, it flexes the joint between the first two segments of its thorax and then snaps it rapidly back into position, often with a loud snapping or clicking sound, from which the beetles get their name. The snap launches the beetle several inches into the air and flips it over so that it lands on its feet.

Should the beetle land upside-down again, it will keep flipping itself until it lands the right way up. This ability

▶ *This is an eyed elater beetle, which lives in eastern North America. It grows to about 1.75 inches (45 mm) long. The species gets its name from the two eyelike spots on its thorax.*

▼ *An illustration of the clicking behavior of a click beetle. Click beetles use this behavior to right themselves.*

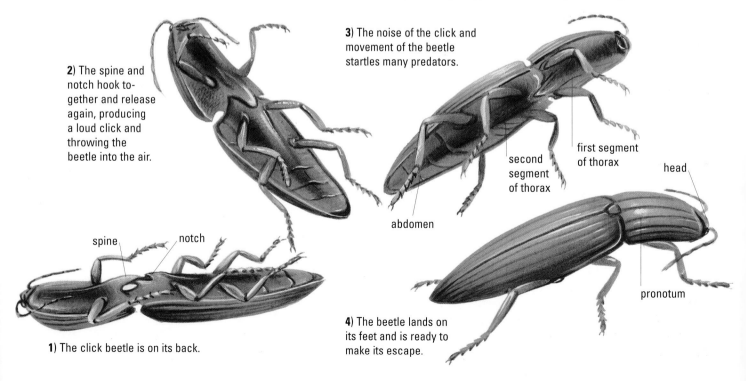

2) The spine and notch hook together and release again, producing a loud click and throwing the beetle into the air.

3) The noise of the click and movement of the beetle startles many predators.

second segment of thorax

first segment of thorax

head

abdomen

spine

notch

pronotum

1) The click beetle is on its back.

4) The beetle lands on its feet and is ready to make its escape.

probably developed to help the beetles to escape from predators, and it is unique among beetles. Small click beetles can snap up to a height of several inches above the ground. Surprisingly, larger species cannot jump as high and can propel themselves only 1 or 2 inches (2.5 or 5 cm) into the air.

If the beetle cannot right itself after a few tries, it will lie still, tucking the antennae and legs in along its sides, and pretend to be dead. If it is picked up, the beetle snaps its body again and again. This behavior startles predators, making them drop the beetle.

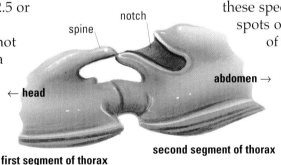

The spine hooks onto the notch. When it is released, the force throws the beetle into the air with a loud click.

first segment of thorax

second segment of thorax

← head

spine

notch

abdomen →

Glowing in the dark

Click beetles that are nocturnal are usually dull brown or black, while many tropical species are active during the daytime and are brightly colored. Some tropical beetles are called lantern click beetles, or cucujos. Adults of these species have luminous spots on the first segment of their thorax and on the underside of their abdomen. These spots are made up of cells known as photocytes, which give out light by reacting a mixture of chemicals inside. The beetles glow when they walk or fly but do not flash like fireflies. The larvae (young

◀ *An illustration of the click mechanism in the thorax.*

143

forms) of these beetles also glow in the dark. The purpose of this luminescence in click beetles is unknown, but it may be used to attract other small insects on which the larvae can then feed.

Eating plants and crops

Adult click beetles feed on small insects, on flowers, or on plant juices. Larval click beetles feed on the young of other insects and sometimes on sprouting seeds and roots. Most are predatory, but some are omnivorous (feed on a variety of different things). The larvae generally go through between three to five molts, and development to full adulthood can take up to three years depending on the availability of food.

The larvae of some species of click beetles are elongated, shiny, and hard. They are called wireworms. Wireworms usually inhabit grasslands where they feed on the roots and underground tubers (storage organs) of plants. However, they can also attack crops such as wheat, corn, and potatoes and are a major economic pest in areas where these crops are grown.

Control of wireworms is difficult. Insecticides are often used to kill the larvae before they can do too much damage. However, managing crops is also important. For example, farmers can reduce the effects of wireworms by

DISTRIBUTION

☐ **EYED ELATER**

making sure that they do not grow potatoes in fields that were previously used for grass crops, such as wheat. In addition, farmers must plow soil well before planting, as this kills the roots and tubers upon which the wireworms live in the absence of tasty crop plants.

Other click beetle larvae are flattened and have a softer body, often with a forked structure at the tip of the abdomen. Most of these species feed on other wood-dwelling insects.

▼ *The metallic sheen of this rain forest click beetle reflects the colors of the leaves in its habitat. It is also possible that the beetles mimic tiny dew drops that are a common feature of the rain forest.*

CLOTHES MOTH

Clothes moths are major pests that have been spread around the world by humans. Their caterpillars feed on natural fabrics and can make holes in clothing.

By hitching a ride on people's clothes, clothes moths have spread around the world, and they are now found wherever people live. Modern clothes are often treated with chemicals to repel moths, but the insects still do an enormous amount of damage.

Adult clothes moths cannot feed because they lack working mouthparts, but the caterpillars more than make up for this by having enormous appetites. They are especially fond of expensive fabrics made from the fibers of animals, including silk, wool, and fur. Unlike most moths, they avoid the light, so they often remain undiscovered until they have caused serious damage. Clothes stored in dark, undisturbed places such as basements, attics, or the back of a closet are most at risk.

As well as munching their way through fur coats and woolen suits, clothes moth caterpillars eat carpets, blankets, upholstery, hair, leather, feathers, and dead insects. Clothes moths belong to a large moth family, the members of which feed on all sorts of decaying matter, including rotting plants, rubbish in birds' nests, and the hair and skin of dead animals.

How to spot a clothes moth

Adult clothes moths are small, straw-colored moths about 0.5 inches (13 mm) long, with a wingspan of 0.5 to 1 inch (13 to 25 mm). There are two main pest species: the case-making clothes moth and the webbing clothes moth. Both have long antennae and a distinct tuft of hairs on their heads. The webbing

▲ *An adult webbing clothes moth on a golden eagle feather.*

clothes moth is a uniform straw color, while the case-making moth has dark specks on the wings and is slightly browner but with paler hairs on its head. A third species, called the carpet moth, also infests clothes and rugs.

If you find moths flying around inside your home, they are probably not clothes moths. Clothes moths are seldom seen and they rarely fly, though they are very good at running. When disturbed, they scurry quickly into dark crevices to hide.

The larvae of clothes moths are creamy white caterpillars with black heads; they grow up to 0.5 inches (13 mm) long. As they crawl about, webbing clothes moth caterpillars secrete feeding tubes made out of silk; this makes it easy to identify which species is present in damaged fabric.

▶ *Case-making moth larvae. These caterpillars use their cases for protection, camouflage, and pupation.*

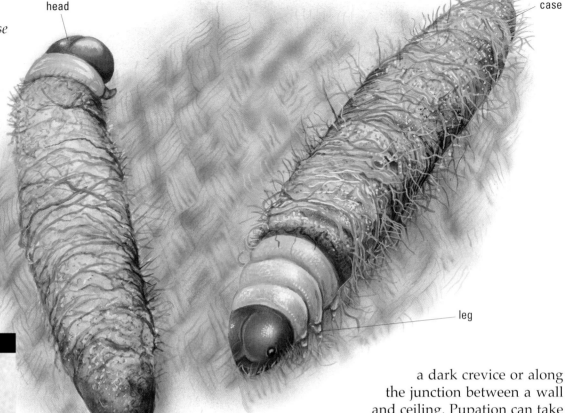

head

case

leg

KEY FACTS

Name
Webbing clothes moth (*Tineidea bisselliella*)

Distinctive features
White caterpillar with black head; silk cases; adult is straw colored

Habitat
Natural fabrics in dark places

Behavior
Adult avoids light, seldom flies but may run; larva feeds on fibers

Breeding
Female lays about 40 eggs on clothes

Food
Wool, silk, fur, feathers, and grime

Size
Adult: 0.5 inches (13 mm) long

The caterpillars of case-making clothes moths live inside a portable case made out of silk woven together with bits of debris and feces. This case is often the same color as the food the caterpillar lives on, which helps disguise it. Case-making clothes moth caterpillars never leave their silky cases and retreat into them when disturbed. The case has enough room inside for the caterpillar to turn around and feed from either end.

The clothes moth life cycle

On average, the life cycle of clothes moths lasts for four to six months, and there are two generations every year. However, the caterpillars can take anything from a month to more than two years to mature, depending on the type of food available and the temperature. The caterpillars molt five times or more as they grow. If they do not eat enough food, they will get smaller with each molt. Finally, they turn into pupae and begin to change into adults, often after crawling away from their food into

a dark crevice or along the junction between a wall and ceiling. Pupation can take place at any time of year in a heated building, taking just more than a week in summer but around a month in winter. Webbing clothes moths spin a case to pupate in, but case-making moths simply seal their existing ones.

The lives of adults are short and almost entirely focused on mating and egg laying. Females live for two to three weeks and usually stay hidden in dark places. They attract males by emitting a chemical called a pheromone, which the males detect with their antennae. The males live longer than the females and are more inclined to fly, especially to find mates. They tend to flutter about rather than flying in a steady direction as other moths do. After mating, females lay an average of 40 to 50 sticky eggs on fabric and then die. The eggs hatch in a week during warm weather.

Controlling these pests

Clothes moths can cause serious damage to clothes in a surprisingly short time, but they are relatively easy to kill and deter without having to resort to insecticides. Infested materials

DISTRIBUTION

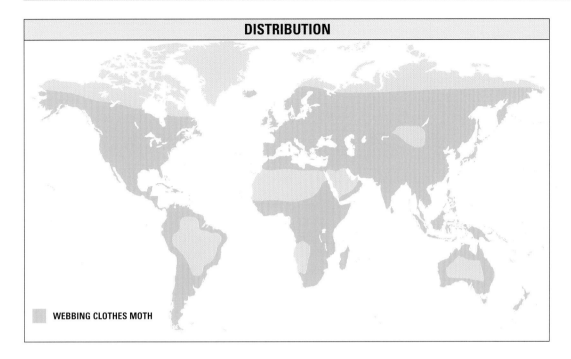

WEBBING CLOTHES MOTH

should be thrown away or washed in hot water if only lightly damaged; any clothes nearby should be thoroughly laundered and closets cleaned out. The chemicals used in dry cleaning are effective at killing any stage of the clothes moth. Clothes moths sometimes infest the edges of woolen carpets where people seldom tread, but they can be removed by vacuuming. Steam cleaning will also kill any stage of the clothes moth. Items that cannot be cleaned can be placed in a freezer for about a week. Items intended for the freezer are placed inside two sealed bags. After treatment, the bags are left closed until they reach room temperature. This stops condensation from spoiling the cloth when the item is removed. Precious fabric can be stored safely in cedar chests or with moth balls. Cedar and moth balls both release vapors that repel the moths.

◄ These webbing clothes moth larvae feed inside a silken cocoon; the remains of some of these can be seen near the top of the photograph.

SEE ALSO

- Gypsy moth
- Hawkmoth
- Metamorphosis
- Moth and butterfly

COCKROACH

Some species of cockroaches are only too familiar to many people. One of the most common of all household pests, these remarkably adaptable insects can infest people's homes and are difficult to remove.

The presence of cockroaches in a house can be unpleasant enough, but their smelly waste products can contaminate food and cause health problems. In some cases, the cockroach may even carry disease-causing viruses or bacteria. Often, insecticides are used in an effort to control insects, but cockroaches have developed immunity to many of these poisonous chemicals. The cockroaches that infest buildings the world over are actually only a few of

▼ *A close-up of an American cockroach. The insect's mouthparts allow it to feed on a wide range of foodstuffs.*

around 4,000 species found worldwide. Many of the very common species of pest cockroaches are not native to the areas where they live. For example, although the American cockroach and the German cockroach are found in America and Germany, they are not native to either country. In fact, they have both been introduced to these and many other countries from warmer, tropical regions, through human activities like shipping and trade. In some cases, it is the presence of artificially heated habitats such as human houses that protects the cockroaches from harsh environmental conditions that would otherwise have killed them.

Classifying cockroaches

Cockroaches belong to the order Blattodea, although they are sometimes grouped together with the praying mantises. There are six families of cockroaches, and representatives of the order live all over the world. Most species are found in forested tropical areas and have no negative impact whatsoever on human activities. In fact, in most places cockroaches are a vital

ANATOMY OF A COCKROACH

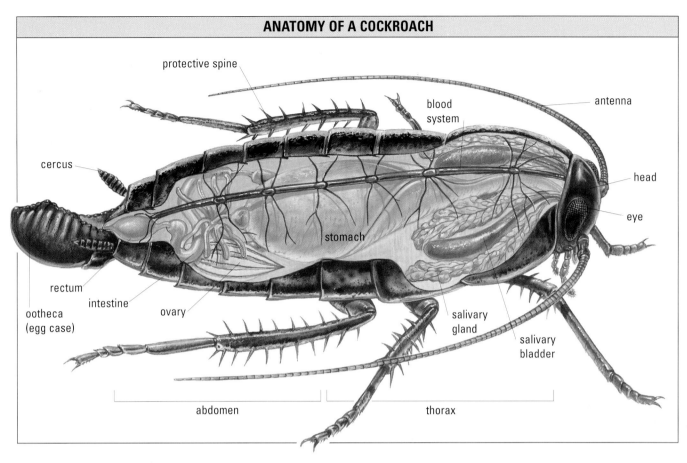

protective spine

blood system

antenna

cercus

head

eye

stomach

rectum

intestine

ovary

salivary gland

salivary bladder

ootheca (egg case)

abdomen

thorax

part of the ecosystem, since they help decompose dead and decaying animal and vegetable matter. They also provide food and hosts for many different predators and parasites.

The cockroach body
Most cockroaches have two pairs of wings. The first pair are thick and leathery. These are held flat over the back, protecting the second, membranous (lacelike) pair. *Megaloblatta longipennis*, a South American cockroach, has the largest wingspan, at up to 8 inches (20 cm). However, several species of cockroaches have no wings as adults.

Cockroaches have an oval-shaped body, and they are generally flattened. Such a body shape allows them to slip into small spaces and narrow cracks. Cockroaches also have a pronounced shieldlike structure, called a pronotum, that lies over most of the back of the head. At the rear end of the abdomen, cockroaches have two pronounced outgrowths, called cerci. Cockroaches

have long antennae that they use for picking up odors and as feelers. They also have vibration-sensitive hairs on their legs, and good vision, which helps the insects cope with many habitats.

Swift runners
Many animals, including lizards, small mammals, spiders, and centipedes prey upon cockroaches. The cockroaches counter this with a range of defenses. Although many cockroaches have wings, not all species fly readily, but when faced with danger, cockroaches usually run away quickly. The cockroach leg is long and slender, allowing it to run swiftly.

However, running away is not the only defense a cockroach has at its disposal. Some species opt for chemical warfare and can produce irritating or smelly chemicals to drive off enemies. The harlequin cockroach can emit a chemical called amyl acetate, which has a smell powerful enough to deter most predators. Other species of cockroaches

▲ *The anatomy of a female cockroach.*

149

Cockroach coprophagy

Cockroaches eat almost anything, including the droppings of other cockroaches. Feeding on feces is termed coprophagy. This behavior is a survival mechanism, allowing the cockroaches to obtain more nutrients from their food. Coprophagy may also help the cockroaches to survive short-term food shortages. Some cockroaches are dependent on microorganisms inside their gut to digest food, and coprophagy allows them to re-establish colonies lost after the insects have molted. This behavior has been used by people trying to control cockroaches in buildings, such as homes and offices. If a cockroach consumes a slow-acting poison, other cockroaches will die after eating the droppings of the contaminated cockroach.

scare away predators by making noises, or by squirting chemicals at them.

Food for thought

Cockroach mouthparts are not specialized to feed on one particular foodstuff. Because of this, cockroaches are able to feed on a very wide range of dead and decaying animal and plant matter.

The cave cockroach feeds on bird or bat droppings, while wood cockroaches feed exclusively on dead wood. To digest their food effectively, these insects have tiny microorganisms living in their gut. These microbes break down the wood, yielding sugars that the cockroaches absorb. However, as with all insects, young wood cockroaches need to molt their outer coverings and stomach linings as they grow. When they molt, cockroaches lose most of their gut microorganisms. To solve this problem, they eat the droppings of other wood cockroaches. Inside the droppings are enough microbes to allow the insects to digest their wood diet once more.

Life cycle and reproduction

Cockroach reproduction involves the use of chemicals. Both male and female cockroaches can attract the attention of a mate using chemical signals. During mating, the male puts a packet of sperm

SEE ALSO
- *Feeding*
- *Metamorphosis*
- *Pest*
- *Praying mantis*

▼ *A wood roach on a plant stem. Wood cockroaches sometimes wander into houses, but they generally die after a few days because, unlike other cockroaches, they need plenty of moisture to survive.*

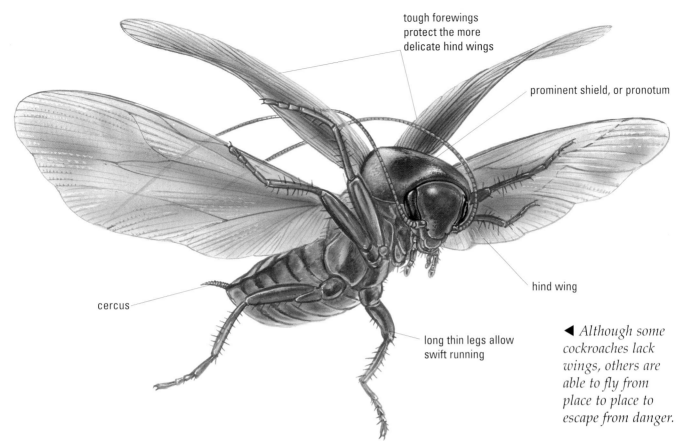

tough forewings protect the more delicate hind wings

prominent shield, or pronotum

hind wing

cercus

long thin legs allow swift running

◀ *Although some cockroaches lack wings, others are able to fly from place to place to escape from danger.*

inside the female. After the eggs are fertilized by the sperm, the female produces an ootheca, or egg case, which contains between 10 and 40 fertilized eggs. Many types of cockroaches deposit the egg case when they find a suitable spot. However, many cockroach species carry the ootheca around, sticking out of their ovipositor (egg tube), until the young are ready to emerge and begin to feed. The young cockroaches, or nymphs, are similar in form to the adults, differing mostly in size and their lack of working wings or sexual organs. Nymphs undergo only a relatively small change in form as they develop through 5 to 12 molts before reaching adulthood.

Well adapted for survival

When living in human houses, cockroaches use all types of crevices and cracks for shelter, making them hard to eliminate. They may simply hide away in small numbers during the day before emerging later. Able to feed on human food, reproduce quickly, develop resistance to several types of chemical

insecticides, and to remain hidden away from view, cockroaches are extremely well adapted to living alongside us in our homes. Some species are now found solely in the houses of people.

▲ *Oriental cockroaches are highly adaptable. They are pests around the world.*

151

COLORADO POTATO BEETLE

The potato beetles are among the best-known and largest members of the leaf beetle family. One species, the Colorado potato beetle, has been introduced into Europe and parts of Asia and is one of the most destructive pests.

There are 31 species of potato beetles, all of which live in the Western Hemisphere, especially Mexico and the southwestern United States. Potato beetles are shiny and round, and most species are between 0.4 and 0.6 inches (10 and 15 mm) long. Some are brightly colored and patterned with black, orange, or even blue. All potato beetle adults and the colorful, plump larvae feed on the leaves of plants in the nightshade family. While most of the plants in this family are very toxic to humans, the tubers of the potato and fruits of the tomato are important human foods.

Potatoes and potato beetles
The most familiar species of potato beetle is the Colorado potato beetle. It is easily recognized by its yellow or pale brown color and ten black stripes on the wing covers. The cultivated potato was first encountered by Europeans in the high Andes Mountains of South America. It was the basic food of the peoples of Peru and Bolivia and had been cultivated in the area for thousands of years.

The Spanish, who first found potatoes in 1532, sent tubers and seeds back to Spain in 1565. By the early 17th century, potatoes were a popular food in much of Europe and had soon spread throughout the continent, to England and eventually Ireland, where they became a major source of food. Later, when European settlers reached the east coast of North America, they brought the potato with them.

A taste for potato
In 1811, not long after the introduction of potatoes to North America, a new species of beetle was discovered feeding on a wild nightshade, buffalo bur, in the Rocky Mountains. At first, the

◀ *A Colorado potato beetle grub in Arizona. Both adults and young feed on the leaves of potatoes, as well as another plant from the same family, buffalo bur.*

DISTRIBUTION

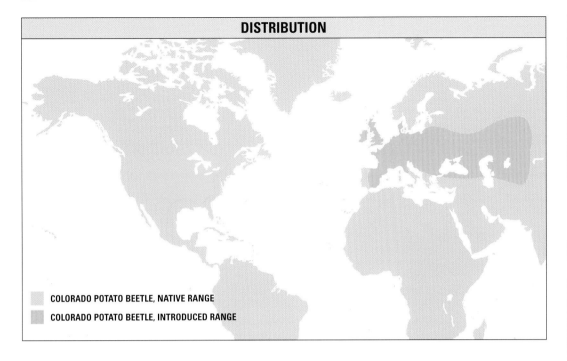

COLORADO POTATO BEETLE, NATIVE RANGE

COLORADO POTATO BEETLE, INTRODUCED RANGE

species was of little interest, but as settlers moved west and introduced potatoes into areas where the beetle was found, the beetles soon began to eat the potatoes with devastating effects.

A major pest

After getting its first taste of potato, the beetle began to spread east rapidly, following the path of the early farmers and wiping out potato crops as it went. By the 1870s, it had reached the Atlantic coast and soon after was accidentally carried across the Atlantic Ocean to Europe. Early efforts to control the Colorado potato beetle involved simply picking the fat, grublike larvae from the leaves of the plants and killing them. Later, insecticides such as DDT were used, but the beetles always seemed to develop resistance. In the last few years, environmental concerns have led to a greatly decreased use of insecticides. A greater emphasis is now placed on finding methods of biological control for these common insects. That is where natural predators or parasites are used to control a pest species.

▶ *The Colorado potato beetle has a distinctive coloration, with ten black bands running along the wing case.*

SEE ALSO

- *Beetle*
- *Biological control*
- *Insecticide*
- *Pest*

KEY FACTS

Name
Colorado potato beetle (*Leptinotarsa decimlineata*)

Distinctive features
Shiny, round, and yellow with ten black stripes on wing case

Food
Adult and larva eat leaves of cultivated potatoes and other members of nightshade family

Range
Originally from Rocky Mountain states but now widespread across North America, Europe, and Central Asia

Breeding
Female lays up to 500 eggs on potato plants; larva grows rapidly in 15 to 20 days; pupal stage lasts 5 to 10 days; two generations per year in warm areas, one generation per year in cool areas

Size
0.3 to 0.4 inches (8 to 10 mm) long

COLORATION

The color world of insects is rich and varied. Insects use colors for many different reasons, such as to hide from predators or to find a mate.

◀ *When it is threatened, this lubber grasshopper reveals its colorful hind wings, startling the predator and allowing the grasshopper to get away.*

two ways. Light reflected from the insect may be changed by scales, ridges, and channels on the body of the insect. These are called structural colors, and different types of ridges and scales produce different colors. They are produced because the waves of light interfere with each other, enhancing the appearance of

Insects generally have good color vision. Most species cannot see the color red very well, but they can see into the ultraviolet (UV) spectrum. UV light is the part of sunlight that is invisible to us but which causes suntans. Many flowers reflect patterns of UV light that are visible to pollinators such as bees. This may be exploited by some spiders, which use UV-sensitive markers on their webs to entice insects. The huge variety of color patterns found in insects is produced in

KEY WORDS

Camouflage
Coloration that helps insect blend into background

Pigment colors
Colors produced by chemicals found in the insect's skin

Sexual coloration
Attracts members of the opposite sex

Structural colors
Colors produced through reflection of light from ridges, scales, and channels on the insect's body

Thermoregulation
How an animal maintains the correct body temperature

Warning colors
Bright coloration, often in stripes of yellow or red and black; warns predators that an insect does not taste good or has a stinger

◀ *Coloration can help insects, such as this moth, merge into the background.*

154

▲ *A weevil from the forests of New Guinea. Insects tend to be more colorful nearer the tropics.*

▶ *The contrasting yellow and black colors of this wasp beetle warn vertebrate predators that it would not make a pleasant meal.*

some colors but diminishing others. The same effect is seen in the colors of soap bubbles, or in a layer of oil on water.

Pigments

Insects also produce colors using pigments. Pigments are chemicals that absorb some parts of sunlight but not others. Pigments can be obtained directly from the insect's diet or can be manufactured by the body. There are many different types of pigments, but common ones include carotenoids, which produce red or yellow colors, bile pigments, which are blue or green, and melanin, which is black or brown.

What is color used for?

Color serves three main purposes in insects: defense against predators, communication with other insects, and controlling body temperature. Predators such as birds use vision, rather than smell or sound, to find insects. Because of this, many insects are leaf colored or look like leaves or twigs to trick predators. Such coloration is an example of camouflage. Like insects, birds can see UV light, so the camouflage has to include light at these wavelengths.

Not all species are camouflaged, though. Some, such as monarch butterflies and bees, are very brightly colored. Although insects like these can easily be seen by vertebrate predators such as birds and mammals, bright colors are associated with poison, a nasty taste, or a stinger, and predators tend to leave brightly colored insects alone. Some insects exploit this by being colored in a similar way to a wasp, for example, despite the fact that they lack any form of stinger. This is called mimicry.

Many insects communicate with color, especially when trying to find a mate. Colors are used in display and courtship. Females are more likely to mate with males that have brightly colored bodies.

Keeping warm through color

Color can also be used to regulate body temperature. Butterflies and other flying insects often bask in the sun or shiver their flight muscles to warm up. Some have hairs to help retain heat. The pigment melanin plays an important role in temperature control. Dark surfaces absorb more heat from the Sun than light ones. Melanin is a dark pigment, so the more melanin an insect has, the greater the amount of heat energy it absorbs. This is why flying insects from colder regions tend to have more melanin, and so appear darker, than species from warmer regions.

COMMUNICATION

Like people, insects and spiders need to communicate with each other for many reasons. Sound, sight, and touch are all important, and signals are sent chemically as pheromones.

Insects use several different methods to communicate with each other. Communication signals must be distinct from the signals used by other species. For example, the dance that a male springtail performs to encourage a female to mate must be correct. If it is not, then the female will not recognize the male as a member of her own species and will not mate with him.

Communicating through touch

Many species of insects feed at night, in the dark, and some even live in pitch-black caves. Touch is a very important sense for these species. Insect antennae are very sensitive touch organs, and they are often used to gather information about other insects nearby. Touch can be used to recognize nest mates. For example, a female mole cricket can

KEY WORDS

Compound eye
Many-lensed eye

Courtship
An interaction between male and female before mating takes place

Mechanoreceptors
Cells in insect skin that allow touch to be used for communication

Pheromone
Chemical signal released by an insect that can attract other insects, warn them away, or suppress reproduction

Ultraviolet light
Short-wavelength light that is invisible to humans and other mammals but is an important part of bird and arthropod vision

◄ *Foraging ants lay a trail of pheromones down, allowing other workers to find the food source.*

recognize her young by touching them with her antennae. Honeybees touch each other to give and receive information when they are crowded together inside the beehive.

Bees that find new sources of food perform a "waggle dance" on the honeycomb after they return to the hive. This dance lets other bees in the colony know exactly where to find the food that it has just returned from. The bee starts by walking in a figure eight. It then walks in a straight line between the two circles, waggling its abdomen as it goes. During the dance, the other bees crowd closely around so that they brush against the dancing bee. The angle of the dance on the honeycomb, and the number of times the dancer waggles its abdomen, inform the crowd of bees which direction to go and how far to fly to find the food source.

Touch is an important part of courtship in spiders. Many male spiders strum a message on the web of female spiders. The message has to be correct, otherwise the female will think it is caused by a trapped insect struggling and may attack the courting male.

Sight
The colors of insects are often an important part of courtship, used to display to potential mates. Insects can even communicate using colors that we cannot see—for example, many butterflies have coloration that can be seen clearly only in ultraviolet (UV) light.

◀ *The bright colors on this swallowtail butterfly communicate that this individual is healthy and would make a good mate.*

Communicating through sound
Sound signals made by an insect are generally used to grab the attention of other individuals of the same species, in particular as an invitation to mate.

Sometimes, the sounds that are made during normal behavior communicate information. The high-pitched whine that the vibrating wings of a mosquito makes as it flies can be heard by others,

▼ *This female hessian fly emits a pheromone from her ovipositor (egg tube) to attract males.*

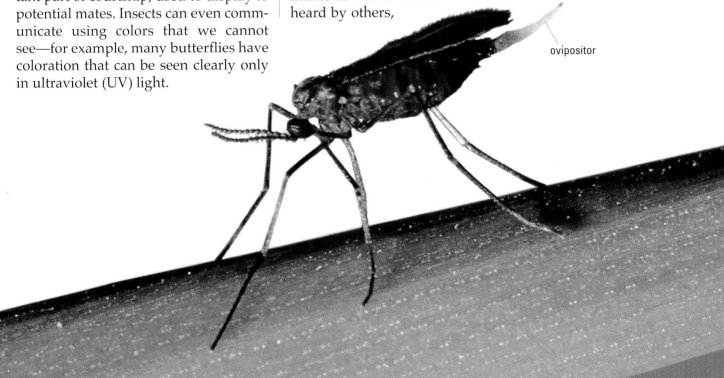

ovipositor

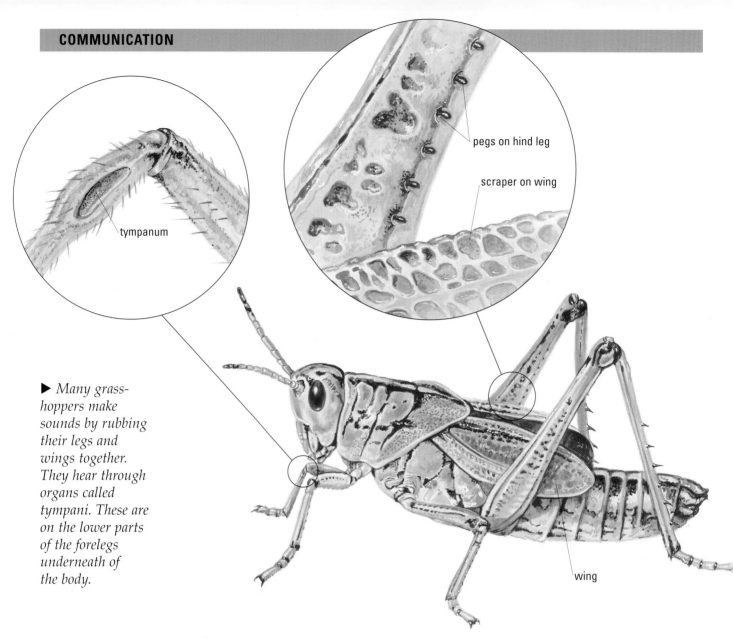

pegs on hind leg

scraper on wing

tympanum

wing

▶ *Many grass-hoppers make sounds by rubbing their legs and wings together. They hear through organs called tympani. These are on the lower parts of the forelegs underneath of the body.*

and this helps males and females to find each other in the dark. Some insects use modified parts of their bodies to make sound. Crickets are more often heard than seen because of the familiar chirping sound they make. They have peglike structures on one wing and a scraper on the other, which make a loud noise when rubbed together.

Grasshoppers also have a scraping technique for making sound, but they rub their wings against their legs instead of each other. As part of their courtship, some bugs rub their front legs on a ridged section of the head, producing a series of loud clicks.

Some species attract mates by striking part of the body against a hard surface. Wood-boring deathwatch beetles hit their heads against the walls of the tunnels in which they live, making sounds that are heard by other beetles.

Chemical communication

Most communication between insects is carried out using chemicals known as pheromones, which are stored in glands inside the insects' bodies. Sometimes,

Sound communication in moths

Although moths generally use pheromones to communicate, some also use sound at a frequency too high for humans to hear. This ultrasound is produced by organs located around the thorax (midbody) and abdomen. These organs help the moth avoid being eaten by bats. Bats hunt by echolocation—bouncing sound off objects to "see" them. Ultrasound signals from the moth confuse the bats, making them "see" things that are not there. However, these sounds have evolved to play an important role in moth courtship.

◀ *When they find a food source, sap beetles release pheromones that attract other beetles in large numbers. By feeding in a group, there is less chance that an individual sap beetle will be caught and eaten by a predator.*

the openings to the gland have hairs that help disperse the chemicals. The pheromones are like a scent language, and often different combinations of chemicals prompt a different response. Scent messages are generally picked up by the antennae, which are often covered by sensitive hairs.

Pheromones have an array of functions. Many insects release them into the air to attract a mate. Some flies lay their eggs inside fruit and leave pheromones to let other flies know that the fruit is occupied.

When threatened, aphids release a warning pheromone. Groups of aphids are generally all females that reproduce without mating. These bugs are genetically identical to their mothers, sisters, and daughters. When an aphid is threatened, it pays to warn all the nearby aphids, since it is likely that they are carrying the same genetic information. The individual aphid may die but its genes stand a better chance of being passed on. Pheromones can betray a hiding place. Some parasitic flies detect bug pheromones, which lead them straight to their eggs.

Pheromones in social insects

In social insects, pheromones control the running of the colony. In a bee hive, pheromones released by the queen bee tell the others what jobs to do. The queen also stops other females from reproducing by using pheromones; if the queen bee dies, this chemical disperses, and another female takes her place. Ants use pheromones as a guide to a food source. A trail is marked with chemicals directing the foraging ants. Similarly, when an ant's or termite's nest is disturbed, alarm pheromones are released, and the insects attack.

Spider pheromones

Pheromones are important for spiders, with many species releasing them into the air. Female wolf spiders lay down pheromone-covered silk trails for the males to follow. Some female spiders build their webs with pheromone-laden silk. When a male sierra dome spider arrives, he immediately pulls down the web and bundles it up; this stops the release of more pheromones, so other males cannot find the female.

◀ *Bees are attracted to flowers by their smell. After feeding, they return to the nest and inform other workers of the flower's position by performing a dance.*

SEE ALSO
• *Ant*
• *Aphid*
• *Bee*
• *Bolas spider*
• *Coloration*
• *Moth and butterfly*
• *Senses*
• *Social insect*
• *Wolf spider*

CRAB SPIDER

These short, wide-bodied predators look a little like crabs. They are masters of disguise and can change their color to match the background. Many crab spiders hunt for pollinating insects on flower heads.

Some crab spiders live on the ground, while others reside on plants. Flower-dwelling species, such as the ridge-faced crab spider, are brightly colored and some can change color to match their backgrounds. Since they have poor eyesight, crab spiders rely on touch to locate prey. More than 1,000 species of crab spiders live worldwide, with 100 species in the United States.

Crab spiders vary in color from shades of brown to bright pink. They have eight small eyes placed in two rows across the front section of their body. Their eight legs are directed sideways at right angles from the body and kept close to the ground. The first two pairs of legs are long and thick, while the remaining pairs are short and slender.

A series of air sacs with many side pockets, called book lungs, draw in oxygen from air. This passes into the body through a spiracle (opening) near the silk-producing spinnerets. There are three pairs of spinnerets, which produce silk for making egg sacs and drag lines.

Courtship, eggs, and spiderlings

Male crab spiders are tiny compared to the larger females and are often a different color. There is little courtship; the male usually just clambers over the female before mating, though some species cover the female in a veil of silk.

Males of some species start guarding females even before they are able to breed, fighting to keep rival males away. The males of a few species are unusual, since they sometimes drink nectar and feed on pollen as well as insects.

DISTRIBUTION

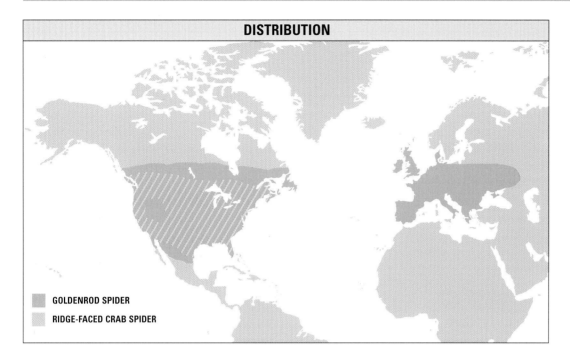

GOLDENROD SPIDER
RIDGE-FACED CRAB SPIDER

Name
Goldenrod spider (*Misumena vatia*)

Distinctive features
Crablike body; bright white or yellow coloration

Habitat
Gardens, fields, and woodland throughout Northern Hemisphere

Behavior
Adult waits for prey in flowers

Food
Insects

Breeding
Chalk-white egg sac with 350 eggs

Size
Male body: 0.1 inches (3 mm); female body: 0.3 inches (8 mm)

After mating, the female settles down to produce an egg sac. This is made of two silken disks fastened together at the edges by more silk. The chalk-white egg sac contains up to 350 eggs. The females of some species guard the eggs, while others leave the eggs to develop alone. The spiderlings hatch in fall and over-winter inside the egg sac. They leave the sac in spring, when conditions are more favorable for feeding. If food is not readily available, the spiderlings may start eating each other.

Spiderlings produce silken draglines that are regularly fastened to the ground or plants for safety. Silk is also used for ballooning, in which the spiderling pays out a strand of silk until it is picked up by the wind. Since they lack wings, ballooning is the only way that spiders can disperse quickly over large areas. Most travel for only a few yards, although spiders have been known to travel for long distances while ballooning, crossing whole oceans to land on distant islands.

◀ *A well camou-flaged crab spider feeds on a stiletto fly. Crab spiders catch their prey by stealth, not by using silk as do many other spiders.*

▶ *Spiders from several other families are referred to as crab spiders. This is a running crab spider. These live on the ground and are generally dull in color.*

Catching prey

Crab spiders do not use webs to catch insects or silk to subdue their prey. Instead, they rely on stealth. Flower-dwelling species wait in blossoms with their long legs pointing forward. They seize unsuspecting bees, beetles, butterflies, and wasps with their powerful forelegs. They then bite their prey at the junction between head and thorax. Large or dangerous insects are quickly subdued by powerful venom. Hanging with their head downward, crab spiders then drink their victim's body fluids.

Camouflage and defense

Crab spiders can match their body color to that of their surroundings. White spiders can switch to yellow and back again. This helps them to avoid detection, both by predators and insect prey.

The dull colors of ground-dwelling crab spiders help them to hide among dead leaves, soil, and under bark. Some species cover themselves in dust or debris. A few crab spiders are disguised as objects, such as fruit, seeds, leaf buds, flowers, and even bird droppings. Crab spiders are preyed upon by toads, lizards, and birds. Ants, beetles, and mantises also consume crab spiders.

Mud dauber wasps fill their nests with crab spiders to feed their young. When attacked, young crab spiders can lose a leg as a defensive measure, replacing it with a smaller, paler leg at the next molt.

Other crablike spiders

There are a number of other families of spiders that bear similarities to crabs. These include the closely related running crab spiders, which have long, camouflaged bodies and legs of a similar length. The selenopid crab spiders are mainly found in tropical areas, although some live in the southern United States. They are large, fast, and active at night, and are common household guests. They have six eyes set in a row along the front of the head. Some huntsman spiders are also called giant crab spiders, and they live in the southern United States, where they often feed on cockroaches in houses.

▶ *A goldenrod spider on a flower. These crab spiders can change their color to suit the background, allowing them to hide from both predators and potential prey.*

CRANE FLY

The crane flies make up the largest family of flies, with at least 14,000 species worldwide and 1,500 species in North America. They often fly around houses and near lights at night.

Crane flies can be seen in summer resting on walls, ceilings, and windows, and they are often found around lights after dusk. Some crane flies resemble daddy longlegs spiders or harvestmen. They are easily distinguished from these long-legged arachnids by having three distinct body regions, as well as one pair of working wings. As in other types of true flies, the second pair of wings have evolved into halteres. Halteres act as balancers, helping the crane fly keep steady while flying. Because of their large size, crane flies are one of the easiest insects on which to see halteres.

Crane fly maggots are called leatherjackets and have thick, tough exoskeletons (outer coverings). Leatherjackets crawl on leaves, rummage on stream bottoms, or tunnel through the soil. Some leatherjackets are pests of crops.

Although crane flies reach their greatest diversity in the tropics, they are also

▼ *Close-up of the head and thorax (midbody) of a* Tipula *crane fly.*

▶ *Mating crane flies. The female will lay up to 1,000 eggs on soil or in leaf litter.*

Name
Crane fly
(Family Tipulidae)

Distinctive features
Slender body; two pairs of wings —one modified into thin halteres; six very long, slender legs

Habitat
Lives around the world, in forests, fields, and streams; some species have aquatic larvae

Food
Adult does not feed; larva feeds on roots, rotten wood, and decaying plant material

Lifespan
One or two generations per year; adults live for up to 2 months

found in a wide range of cooler habitats, ranging from sea level to mountain tops up to 16,500 feet (5,600 m) high.

Mating and reproduction

Upon emerging from the pupa, female crane flies already have their full complement of between 70 and 1,000 eggs. Males mate with the females as they emerge from the pupa, or search for mates by flying or walking over the ground, up tree trunks, or on vegetation. Some females find their partners in dense swarms of male flies, mating in midair before settling to the ground or on vegetation. Both sexes may mate more than once.

The eggs are laid soon after mating and hatch within a few days. Typically, they are smooth and dark. Some species

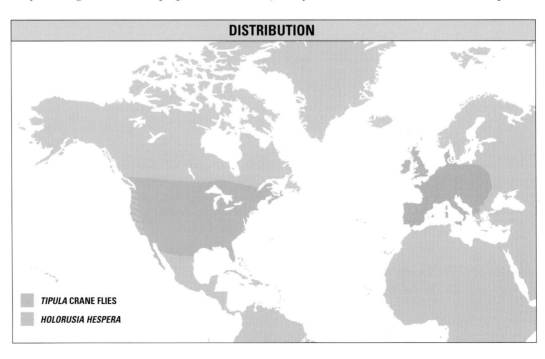

DISTRIBUTION

■ *TIPULA* CRANE FLIES
■ *HOLORUSIA HESPERA*

drop their eggs while in flight. Others lay their eggs on the surface of streams, leaving them to sink to the bottom. Most crane flies deposit eggs as they fly over wet soil, mud, or mats of algae (tiny, plantlike organisms). In species that lay their eggs in dry soils or rotten wood, the female inserts her abdomen and injects her eggs through a long egg tube, or ovipositor.

Aquatic leatherjackets feed on decomposing plant material, algae, and other microscopic plant life. Crane fly larvae are sometimes important in the breakdown and recycling of leaf litter. The larvae of one California species feed on roots. They can strip entire hillsides of grass, and they can also become a pest of grain crops and alfalfa.

Becoming an adult

Leatherjackets usually pupate after the fourth molt, although some species may molt five or more times. The pupa resides inside the last larval skin. Adults later emerge inside the pupa and use spines to burrow through soil, moss, or decayed vegetable matter. Both the pupa and the adult must use the breathing apparatus of the previous life stage to survive. Eventually, the adult emerges from the pupa.

Most crane flies living in temperate regions produce one or two generations per year, although species living in cooler climates may take four or five years to become adults.

Adult crane flies are diverse in both size and habit. The largest species of fly in North America, *Holorusia hespera*, is found west of the Rockies. The female's body length reaches 1.4 inches (36 mm). In spite of a 3-inch (76-mm) wingspan, she is a weak flier. The larvae are 2 inches (51 mm) long and burrow among the roots of stream vegetation or on the bottom of small pools. By contrast, snow flies are only 0.15 to 0.2 inches (4 to 5 mm) long. These tiny, wingless crane flies appear in the snow in early spring, and they are found from New York state to British Columbia.

Defense against predators

Crane flies use a variety of defensive strategies. Many species readily shed their legs when attacked, while others assemble into swarms for protection. Although many die, enough survive to reproduce. The wings of some crane flies may be dark or striped, making them difficult to see. A few species hang from the nonsticky threads of spiderwebs, where they mimic twigs. This provides protection from ants and other invertebrate predators. Some Australian crane flies are colored to mimic stinging wasps, and this deters most predatory birds and mammals.

▲ *A crane fly rests on the trunk of a tree. These large insects are often seen resting on the walls and ceilings of houses.*

SEE ALSO
- *Daddy longlegs spider*
- *Fly*
- *Harvestman*
- *Larva, nymph, and pupa*

DADDY LONGLEGS SPIDER

These spiders are cunning hunters that live in quiet, dark places. Found all over the world, they are able to catch and eat many other arthropods, including other spiders.

There are around 350 species of daddy longlegs spiders living around around the world. One of the most familiar is the European daddy longlegs spider. It is around 0.3 inches (8 mm) long and pale yellow. The abdomen may have markings in a V-shaped pattern.

As in other spiders, the head and thorax (midbody) of daddy longlegs spiders are fused into one section, called the cephalothorax, upon which are located eight eyes. Two triangular sets of three eyes are positioned on the sides, with two smaller eyes located at the front above the mouthparts.

As the name suggests, these spiders have very long legs, which can be up to six times the length of the body. This makes them look similar to harvestmen, although they are not closely related. Daddy longlegs spiders are easily distinguished from harvestmen since they have two distinct body segments, as opposed to one. Crane flies, flying insects with three body segments, are also sometimes called daddy longlegs.

Daddy longlegs are sometimes called cellar spiders, after the dark, damp places where they like to build their untidy webs. The webs consist of strands of nonsticky silk, and are often spun near the ceiling or high in the rafters. The spiders hang upside down near the center of the web.

Spider eaters
European daddy longlegs will feed on just about anything that blunders into their web, including other spiders. They throw silk lines over their prey until it is unable to move before closing in to bite, paralyze, and feed on their catch.

Daddy longlegs often invade the webs of spiders of other species. Not only will they steal a spider's prey and eat its eggs, they will often attack the spider

▲ *The legs of these spiders may be six times longer than the body. The hind pair are used to wrap their prey in silk.*

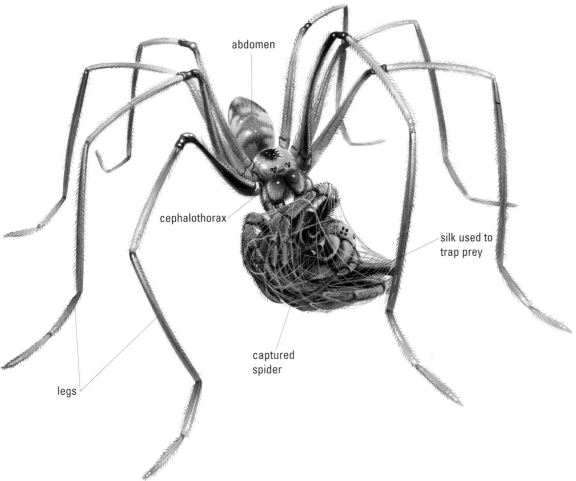

abdomen

cephalothorax

silk used to trap prey

captured spider

legs

◀ *Daddy longlegs spiders throw sheets of silk at their prey from short range. When the prey, such as another spider, is unable to move, the daddy longlegs closes in.*

KEY FACTS

Name
Daddy longlegs spider (*Pholcus phalangioides*)

Distinctive features
Very long and slender legs

Habitat
Dark, damp, and undisturbed places

Behavior
Defensive whirling in web; may attack other spiders or steal their prey

Breeding
Female binds eggs together with silk and carries them in fangs

Food
Insects and other spiders

Distribution
Worldwide

SEE ALSO

- Feeding
- Jumping spider
- Orb-web spider
- Spider
- Wolf spider

itself. Daddy longlegs lure the spider by vibrating their abdomens on the web to mimic the struggles of prey. As the other spider approaches, the daddy longlegs raises itself up on its legs, remaining motionless until the other spider makes contact with its leg. The daddy longlegs then attacks with sheets of silk.

Occasionally, a daddy longlegs will get caught in the web of another spider. When this happens, it chews away the sticky piece attached to its foot and carefully cleans its legs.

Defensive whirling

Although daddy longlegs are fierce predators, their fangs are too small to pierce the skin of a human. If disturbed while in their web, these spiders will tremble and shake the web and spin around so rapidly they become blurry and difficult to see. This whirling behavior probably protects the spider from predatory animals that may try to pluck the spider from its web.

Egg carriers

During courtship, the male cautiously approaches the female, faintly vibrating her web with his abdomen and eventually embracing her with his legs. After mating, the female lays a batch of eggs that she binds together with a few threads of silk. She carries the bundle in her chelicerae (fangs) for around three weeks until the eggs hatch. For the next nine days or so, the spiderlings remain in their mother's web. After this, they molt and proceed to make their own webs around the fringes of the female's web, creating a large tangle of silk.

The spiderlings molt five times over a period of several months as they grow; then they begin to breed themselves. After reaching adulthood, they might live for another two years.

DEATHWATCH BEETLE

The larvae of deathwatch beetles bore through dead dry wood and can feed on furniture in the house. The sounds produced by the adults were once thought to be a sign of an approaching death.

Deathwatch beetles are drab-colored beetles that grow to around 0.2 inches (5 mm) in length. The head is relatively large but is usually tucked under a hoodlike shield extending from the thorax (midbody) and so is not visible from above. These beetles have short legs and often pull them close alongside the body and pretend to be dead when they are disturbed.

Many species are hairy or have tufts of long hair. Some look like bird droppings. There are about 1,600 species in the world, and 300 of these live in North America. Unlike most other beetles, which have more species in tropical areas, deathwatch beetles are far more common in cooler regions.

A boring life

Adults are found on vegetation and dead wood, and some are attracted to lights at night. Larvae (young forms) of some species bore into dead dry wood, especially furniture and the floors, beams, and walls of old houses. For this reason, they are often called woodworm and can be serious pests. Infestations usually start in old furniture before spreading. The larvae riddle the wood with tunnels, causing it to weaken and sometimes to collapse.

A number of species, such as the cigarette beetle and the drugstore beetle, are pests of stored plant products. Drugstore beetles lay their eggs singly in their food source. The larvae feed for four to five months before pupating. While they feed mostly on bread, they

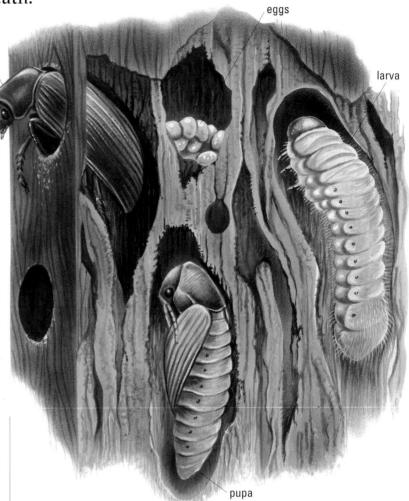

can also be found in flour and cereals. As their name suggests, cigarette beetles feed on the dried tobacco leaves used to make cigarettes.

Infesting trees

Larvae of nonpest species infest twigs, seeds, galls (bumps of leaf tissue produced on the stems and branches of many plants), and sometimes fungi. Larvae of these beetles can take up to five years to develop. This is generally because dead wood is not a very

▲ *The life cycle of a deathwatch beetle. The female lays eggs inside dead wood. The larvae hatch out and eat their way into the timber. The larvae pupate close to the surface. New adults bore their way out before dispersing to find mates.*

DISTRIBUTION

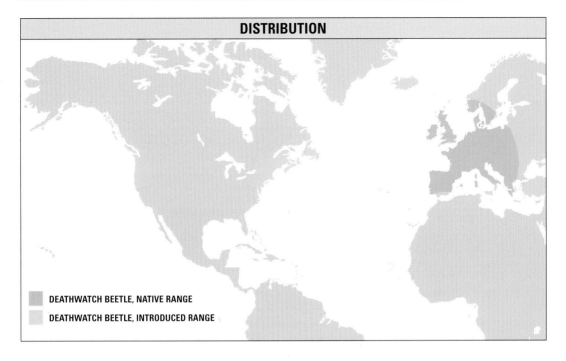

- DEATHWATCH BEETLE, NATIVE RANGE
- DEATHWATCH BEETLE, INTRODUCED RANGE

KEY FACTS

Name
Deathwatch beetle
(*Xestobium
refuvillosum*)

**Distinctive
features**
Head covered by
large shield;
clubbed antennae

Distribution
Native to Europe,
introduced to parts
of North America

Lifespan
Adult lives for a
month; larva takes
one to three years
to develop

SEE ALSO

- *Beetle*
- *Carpet beetle*
- *Pest*

nutritious food. To make up for the lack of nutrition in the wood, the larvae have baglike structures called mycetomes. These are attached to the grubs' digestive systems and contain microscopic organisms that aid in food digestion and supply additional nutrients not found in the wood. Larvae of other wood-boring beetles and other insects have similar pockets of microorganisms.

Knocking on wood

For species that tunnel or burrow, it can be very difficult to meet other beetles for breeding. Several types of deathwatch beetles overcome this problem by communicating with sound. During the mating season, the adults communicate by knocking the lower part of the front of the head against the hard surface they are standing on. This produces a loud rapping sound, often in patterns of seven to eleven beats. Superstitious people once believed that these sounds were caused by a clock counting down the time before a death in the house. This was how the beetles came to be given their common name.

▼ *After emerging, adult females disperse to find new timbers in which to lay eggs.*

DEFENSE

Insects are always under threat of being eaten. To stay alive, insects have evolved a variety of defensive mechanisms, involving poisons and stings, warning colors, chemicals, and mimicry.

◀ *This Malaysian flower mantis is well camouflaged. Interestingly, this insect is on a bougainvillea plant, which has been introduced to the area from overseas. Nonetheless, the mantis is still able to hide among its petals.*

Insects and their relatives have evolved an amazing variety of ways to defend themselves against their enemies. These include making defensive barriers, disguising themselves as leaves or twigs, impersonating other animals, or even using chemical warfare. Predators come in all shapes and sizes, from other insects to birds and mammals. In addition, parasites also pose a constant threat. For example, many parasitic wasps specialize in laying their eggs inside the bodies of insects and spiders.

Defensive strategies

Sometimes, the aim of defensive behavior is to avoid a predator in the first place. Plant-eating insects often hide on the underside of leaves, where they are less noticeable. The larvae of many beetles live relatively safely within trees and dead wood, or feed hidden underground on roots.

Many insects can run, fly, or jump to escape danger. Others, such as caterpillars and many aphids, lack wings and are too slow to outrun predators. If attacked, some caterpillars drop from the leaves where they are feeding and hang onto a silken thread, climbing back up again when the danger has passed. Plant-feeding beetles such as weevils may drop to the ground, where they lie still to escape attention.

The insect body itself may also provide protection. Beetles have thick exoskeletons (hard skins) that small

▶ *Many butterflies have eye patches on their wings. When attacked, these "eyes" make the predator think the butterfly is part of a much larger animal, allowing the insect to escape.*

predators find difficult to penetrate. Caterpillars are often hairy, which deters some birds as well as many insect predators and parasites.

Using color for defense

Color and appearance are often used to mislead birds and other predators that hunt by sight. Many insects are colored to blend in with the background. For this reason, many insects that feed on plants are green. A different form of disguise is disruptive coloration, in which a strong pattern on the body makes it difficult to recognize the overall shape of the insect.

Disguises can also be more specific. Some insects have evolved to look remarkably similar to leaves, complete with imitation fungus spots. Others, such as walking sticks and inchworm caterpillars, imitate twigs and sticks, many hoppers look like thorns, and some spiders closely resemble the droppings of birds. Such disguises work best if the animal keeps still, and they are often used by nocturnal species, which are inactive by day.

Pupal stages of insects may also gain protection in this way. For example, many butterfly chrysalises hang from plants looking like withered leaves.

Flash or startle patterns can disturb a predator. Many butterflies have patterns on their wings that resemble a pair of large eyes. When threatened by a predator (such as a bird), the butterfly opens its wings to reveal the eyes. Often, these eyes look like those of an owl; in the confusion, the butterfly has a few seconds in which to flutter away.

Some grasshoppers and moths have colored hind wings that are visible only during flight, so when the insect lands it seems to disappear.

Mimicry

Mimicry, in which one animal evolves to look like another, is used by many species of insects. Some spiders are mimics as well. In the tropics, a number of spiders mimic ants, mainly as a defense against spider-hunting wasps. However, spiders lack antennae. They solve this problem by raising their front legs to imitate the ant antennae, and they walk on six legs rather than eight. They have even evolved to run like an ant. These spiders live near the insects they mimic, but they rarely prey on them and will avoid close encounters. Many bugs and beetles also mimic ants, as do the nymphs of some species of leaf insects and mantids.

▲ *Damage to a Formosan termite nest brings workers scurrying to repair the breach and soldiers (with darker heads) to repel attackers.*

DISTRIBUTION

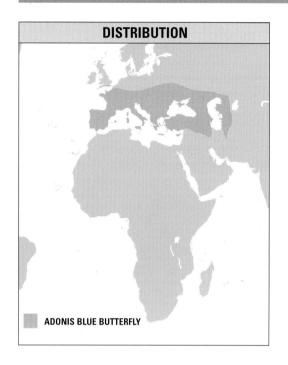

ADONIS BLUE BUTTERFLY

How the adonis blue butterfly hires ants

The adonis blue lives in dry areas with short grass where the caterpillars feed on horseshoe vetch. They attract several different species of ants by producing sounds that resemble ant communications and also by secreting a sweet-tasting fluid that the ants use as a highly nutritious food, rich in proteins and sugars. The ants attend to the caterpillar while it feeds, and they protect it from predators and parasites. At night, the caterpillar returns to ground level, and the ants often bury it in loose soil to keep it safe, sometimes posting a guard overnight.

The ants construct cells for the caterpillar to molt in, and it pupates inside the ants' nest. Like the caterpillars, the pupae communicate with the ants using sound from within the chrysalis. When the adult emerges, it makes its way through the ants' nest to the surface. There, it unfolds its wings and waits until it is warm enough to flutter away.

Many other blue butterflies have close relationships with ants. Some caterpillars are carnivorous and manage to feed on ant-protected aphids by secreting a protein-rich, sugary fluid for the ants to feed on. The ants then let the caterpillar feed on the aphids; the aphids have paid for protection with honeydew but are still preyed upon nonetheless.

▼ *Look closely and you will see a jumping spider, superbly camouflaged on the leaf as a bird dropping.*

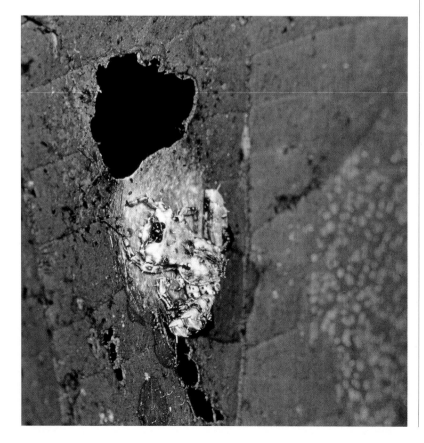

Bright colors are often used to warn predators that an insect is unpleasant to eat. Many brightly colored insects, such as ladybugs and monarch butterflies, store poisons in their bodies. They may take these poisons from the plants on which they feed or make them in their own bodies. Caterpillar hairs serve to irritate predators, and may contain poisonous substances, while some spiders such as tarantulas release tiny hairs that irritate the eyes and skin of vertebrate attackers.

Poisonous species are often mimicked by insects that lack defensive toxins. Groups of some bugs walk along in single file. They resemble a poisonous caterpillar, but this deception works only if the bugs keep together.

Chemical defense

Some arthropods, including many millipedes, bugs, and beetles, have glands that secrete or squirt distasteful or toxic chemicals when they are attacked.

The bombardier beetle squirts a very hot cocktail of chemicals at an attacker, while many bugs secrete smelly chemicals. Some insects produce chemical odors that are not harmful in themselves but are used as a warning to predators that the insect is poisonous.

Building a barrier

Insects often construct shelters or barriers against attack. Many bugs can produce waxy resin threads that are used to build a protective shelter. The underwater larvae of many caddis flies build intricate cases around their bodies, dragging these with them as they move. Many caterpillars live in rolled-up leaves tied with silk, while tent caterpillars live in large colonies protected by silk webs.

The plant-eating larvae of small flies and wasps often cause swellings on plants called galls, which provide both food and protection. Young stages of some froghoppers live on plants within a mass of frothy bubbles, called spittle.

Defense in social insects

Social insects such as ants and termites have elaborate defensive systems for their large nests. The large soldiers deter attackers by biting or stinging them or by plugging the entrance holes with their own heads. Bees and wasps have painful stingers for attacking predators. These insects also signal to each other that their nest is being attacked by releasing alarm pheromones. Aphids are not usually considered social insects, but some species have a similar caste of soldiers. Aphid soldiers are unable to

reproduce and live only to defend other aphids on the plant to which the soldiers are genetically identical. The soldiers have horns, bumps, and spines with which they butt predators such as ladybugs and lacewing nymphs. They can also spread alarm pheromones onto the body of the attacker. When it moves toward the other aphids, they are alerted by the pheromones and can move away to safety.

Ant bodyguards

Aphids and many other insects enlist the protection of ants, which defend them against predators and parasitic wasps and flies. The ants benefit by drinking a sweet liquid, honeydew, that these insects secrete from glands in the abdomen. The caterpillars of many blue butterflies have an even closer relationship with ants: some may even grow up inside the ants' nest, where they might feed on the ant's eggs and larvae.

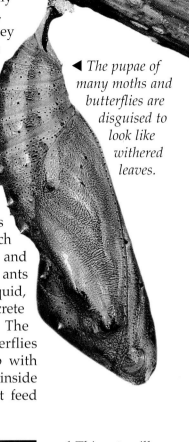

◀ *The pupae of many moths and butterflies are disguised to look like withered leaves.*

◀ *This caterpillar is brightly colored to warn predators that it is poisonous. This will not deter parasitic wasps, however, and the caterpillar combats them by having a coating of fine hairs.*

SEE ALSO

- *Ant*
- *Aphid*
- *Blue butterfly*
- *Bombardier beetle*
- *Coloration*
- *Mimicry*
- *Parasitic wasp*
- *Social insect*
- *Spider wasp*

DISEASE CARRIER

Hundreds of millions of people are affected every year by diseases carried by arthropods, and many millions of these people will die from these diseases.

Many diseases are caused by tiny microorganisms that invade parts of the body, such as the blood system, gut, or brain, making the victim feel unwell and maybe even killing them. Such disease-causing agents are called pathogens, and many are passed between their victims by insects.

Pathogens carried by insects include bacteria, viruses, protists (single-celled organisms), and roundworms. Some insects transfer these disease-causing agents to people through physical contact. If a fly feeds on excrement before visiting a kitchen, for example, it may pass some pathogens on to food.

Most pathogens that are carried by insects, however, are transmitted to humans or animals in either the saliva or feces of blood-sucking insects. Some diseases, such as malaria, are passed on to new individuals only when the right species of biting insects carry the pathogen (a protist, in this case) from infected to uninfected people. Many insect-borne diseases are carried from animal hosts to humans by insects. Other insect-borne diseases affect animals but not people.

The first half of the 20th century saw major advances in the control of insect-borne diseases, partly thanks

◄ *This diagram illustrates the life cycle of the worms that cause river blindness disease. The worms are carried by black-flies, which breed in and live near fast-running streams.*

2) If the blackfly carrying the worms bites another person, he or she may be infected with the worms.

larvae

3) The larvae grow into tiny worms that can cause itching and swelling.

adult worms

1) When a blackfly feeds on the blood of a person suffering from river blindness, the worms that cause the disease pass into the fly's gut.

dead worms

4) If the tiny worms enter the person's eye, allergic reactions to dead worms can cause blindness.

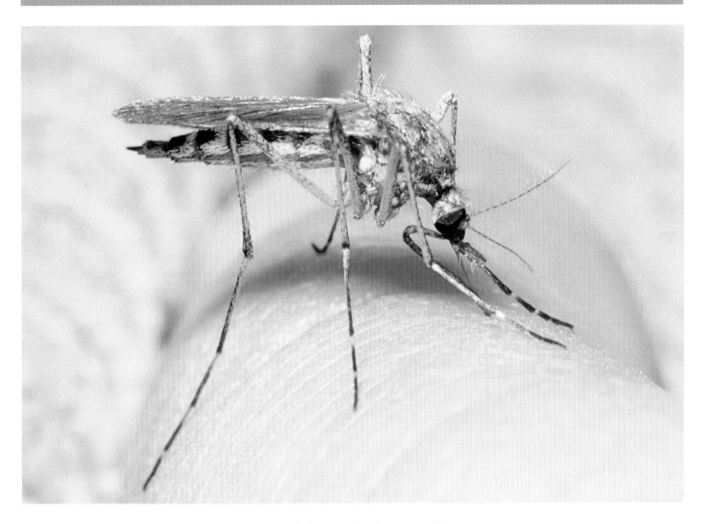

Mosquito-borne diseases

to the use of artificial insecticides, such as DDT, to control disease-carrying insects. Recent years, however, have seen increases in some of the most devastating insect-borne diseases in the tropics and more frequent outbreaks in milder regions.

Growing human populations, changes in agricultural practices, poverty, war, and increased international travel have all contributed to the spread of insect-borne disease. Also, many insect species have developed resistance to insecticides, while some pathogens have developed resistance to the drugs used to treat infected people.

Even relatively disease-free areas, such as Canada and the northern United States, sometimes have outbreaks of diseases introduced from abroad, such as the mosquito-borne West Nile virus, or diseases that normally affect other animals such as bubonic plague.

Many diseases are transmitted by mosquitoes. More than 100 million people contract the weakening and deadly disease malaria every year. Bird malaria, spread in Hawaii by introduced mosquitoes, has resulted in the extinction of many species of birds.

Yellow fever, dengue, and dengue hemorrhagic fever are all caused by viruses. The yellow fever mosquito is the most important carrier of these diseases in urban areas. This mosquito probably moved from Africa to the Americas with the slave trade. Yellow fever epidemics killed thousands of workers during the construction of the Panama Canal.

Dengue fever, which is painful but not usually fatal, is widespread in warmer parts of the world, and epidemics have occurred in the southern United States and Puerto Rico. Dengue hemorrhagic

▲ *A species of mosquito that can carry the pathogen for yellow fever sucks blood from a human finger.*

175

▼ *The mouthparts of a blood-sucking deer tick seen through a very powerful electron microscope. These spiderlike arthropods can infect the people they bite with Lyme disease, a flulike illness caused by bacteria.*

fever, a life-threatening disease, was first identified in 1954. It has been spreading since the mid-1970s.

Other mosquito-borne viruses, including West Nile virus and some kinds of encephalitis, normally occur in birds and can occasionally cause epidemics in humans where certain mosquitoes are common. West Nile virus recently arrived in North America, and it has caused several deaths. An epidemic of St. Louis encephalitis in 1975 resulted in 171 deaths in the United States.

The term *filariasis* covers several diseases that can be transmitted by mosquitos, and are caused by types of roundworms. Elephantiasis is a type of filariasis that causes extreme swelling.

Other insect-borne diseases

River blindness, also called onchocerciasis, is caused by a tiny roundworm carried by blackflies. Allergic reactions to the worms as they die inside a person's eyes can cause blindness. Although most of the millions of people with this disease live in Africa, it also occurs in parts of Central America.

Sleeping sickness, or trypanosomiasis, is another devastating disease caused by a protist that can lead to comas and death. It is transmitted by the bite of tsetse flies in Africa, affecting both humans and livestock such as cattle.

Chagas' disease, which affects the heart and nervous system, is spread in the feces of blood-sucking assassin bugs in South America. Leishmaniasis is a serious disease caused by protists, which are spread from dogs and rodents to people by blood-sucking sand flies. Symptoms can include tissue damage such as ulcers both inside and outside the body. Bubonic plague is caused by a bacterium transmitted from rodents to humans by fleas. A few cases occur each year in the United States, usually in rural areas. Outbreaks of this disease have caused catastrophe through the ages; the collapse of western European civilization during the 6th century probably followed a widescale epidemic. The disease was also responsible for the Black Death, which killed one-third of the population of Europe in the 14th century.

Rickettsia are bacteria-like microorganisms that can only multiply inside the cells of other organisms. Various forms of the disease typhus are caused by rickettsia carried from person to person by lice, especially in cool areas where heavy clothing is worn. Large-scale outbreaks of typhus, which can lead to kidney failure, heart failure, and infections of the blood and lungs, have declined over recent years as standards of hygiene have improved.

Ticks and mites

Many diseases are borne by small arthropods other than insects, especially ticks and mites. Rocky mountain spotted fever, a disease that involves a fever and a bleeding rash and which occurs in both North and South America, is caused by a rickettsia organism transferred from small mammals to people by tick bites.

Some types of typhus are spread by mites, which are small relatives of spiders. Lyme disease causes severe flulike symptoms and is widespread in the United States. Caused by a bacterium, it is spread by the bite of ticks that usually live on deer.

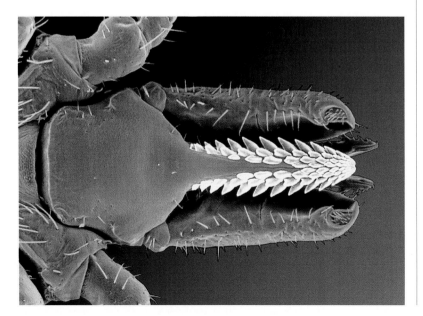

DOBSONFLY

The males of many species of dobsonflies have extremely long mandibles. These are used for fighting with other males during the breeding season.

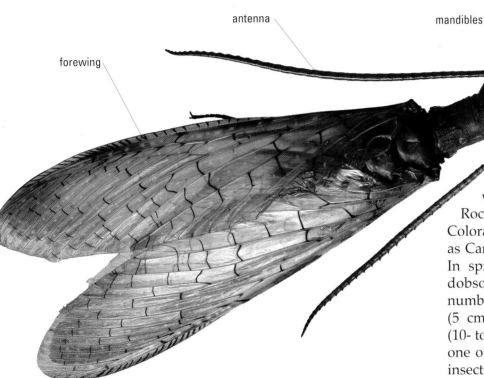

antenna
forewing
mandibles

Corydalus cornutus, lives in the United States. It is widely distributed east of the Rockies and is also found in Arizona, Colorado, and Utah. It lives as far north as Canada and as far south as Panama. In spite of its wide distribution, this dobsonfly is rarely found in large numbers. With a body up to 2 inches (5 cm) long, and with a 4- to 5-inch (10- to 12.5-cm) wingspan, *C. cornutus* is one of the largest and most impressive insects in North America.

Closely related to the alderflies, dobsonflies are remarkable because the males often have very long, prominent mouthparts. The aquatic larvae of dobsonflies, known as hellgrammites, are equally striking and are prized by fishers as bait. Their tough bodies continue to wriggle after being hooked, and they are good for attracting trout and bass. Adult dobsonflies do not feed, but hellgramites prey upon a range of small aquatic animals.

Dobsonflies have two pairs of wings interlaced with veins. The hind wings are broad at the base and are folded up like a fan beneath the long, gray forewings, which are often sprinkled with white spots.

Thirty species of dobsonflies have been identified in the Americas. However, only one species of dobsonfly,

▲ *A male* Corydalus *dobsonfly. The hind wings are protected beneath the forewings. Despite the fearsome mandibles, dobsonflies are harmless to humans.*

▶ *A larval dobsonfly, or hellgrammite. These aquatic insects live under stones, and their presence is an indication of a clean, pollution-free stream.*

Formidable mouthparts

The crossed, tusklike mandibles of the male are nearly half as long as the body and are sharply pointed at the tips.

KEY FACTS

Name
Corydalus cornutus
(no common name)

Distinctive features
Large insect; male has crossed tusklike mandibles

Habitat
Larva lives in cold, clear, fast-moving streams

Lifespan
Larva lives for two or three years; adult lives for one week

DISTRIBUTION

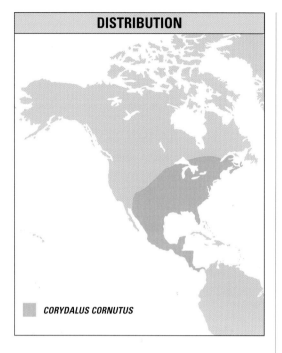

▨ *CORYDALUS CORNUTUS*

▼ *Female dobsonflies, such as this one, have much smaller mandibles than the males.*

Males use these long mandibles in courtship and in competition with other males. In spite of the formidable appearance of the males, it is the shorter, more powerful mandibles of the female that can deliver the most painful bite. However, dobsonflies only bite when

they are carelessly handled. The females lay their eggs near water, typically on the leaves of trees overhanging cold, clear, fast-moving streams, or on rocks or bridges above the waterline.

The egg mass is covered in a chalky white material and is about the size and shape of a nickel. Each egg mass consists of three or more layers with a total of up to 3,000 transparent eggs. The eggs turn gray as they develop. Upon hatching, the hellgrammites immediately drop down into the water below.

Underwater larvae

Hellgrammites are long, flat, dark gray larvae that reach up to 3.5 inches (90 mm) long. Their head has strong mouthparts for chewing, threadlike antennae, and poorly developed eyes. Three pairs of powerful legs are located on the thorax (midbody).

Dobsonfly larvae usually live in fast flowing, oxygen-rich streams, and they can survive the stream drying up for some time. They generally live under stones and will sometimes fight for their homes; however, recent research has shown that when predatory fish are in the same area, the larvae will share their stones with each other. Hellgrammites are active predators, and they feed by sucking up the body fluids of their prey through a hollow tube formed by a groove on the inside of their mouthparts.

The finger-like gills are located on the abdomen of the larva. They absorb oxygen from the surrounding water. The spiracles (air-breathing holes) of hellgrammites remain closed until they leave the water to pupate. Hellgrammites can swim backward and forward using undulating motions of the body as they hunt along the stream bottom. *C. cornutus* mainly preys on

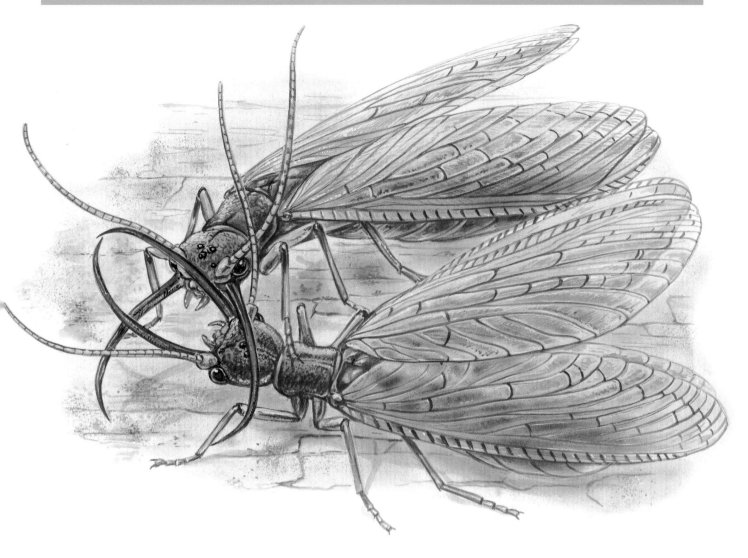

other insects, such as the larvae of net-casting caddis flies, mosquitoes, and blackflies. They sometimes feed on smaller members of their own species.

Pupation in dobsonflies

Hellgrammites may go through as many as 10 or 11 molts, and some species take up to three years to mature. Mature hellgrammites scramble out of the water at night during the late spring and early summer. Many insects spin a silken cocoon in which to pupate, but a hellgrammite will dig a chamber in the soil instead. This chamber can be 30 feet (9 m) or more from the stream. The chambers are generally around 2 to 4 inches (5 to 10 cm) deep and are found beneath stones or logs, or sometimes in decaying driftwood. The pupae are light yellow, with well-developed mandibles projecting forward. They are relatively mobile and are able to give a strong defensive bite to intruders.

A short adult life

Around two weeks later, the adults emerge from their chambers. They rest on streamside vegetation during the day and are seldom seen. Dobsonflies are weak fliers, becoming active mostly at dusk or at night.

The adults do not generally eat solid food, although they occasionally sip nectar or other sweet liquids. Both sexes live for only a week or so as adults, and breeding must take place quickly. Rival males establish territories and fight each other with their mandibles. The females are attracted to males by airborne chemicals called pheromones and sperm is passed to them in sticky capsules.

▲ *Two male dobsonflies wrestle with their large mandibles for the right to mate with females.*

SEE ALSO

- *Alderfly*
- *Ant lion*
- *Dragonfly and damselfly*
- *Lacewing*
- *Mayfly*
- *Sponge fly*

DRAGONFLY AND DAMSELFLY

There are more than 5,000 species of dragonflies and damselflies worldwide. An ancient group, these insects can be very colorful, and they are expert fliers.

◄ *Damselflies laying eggs. The male remains attached to the female as she slowly moves below the surface of the water, laying her eggs on submerged vegetation.*

KEY FACTS

Name
Blue-ringed dancer damselfly (*Argia sedula*)

Distinctive features
Female brown; male black and blue; wings held together over body at rest

Habitat
Rivers and streams

Food
Adult eats small flying insects; nymph eats aquatic insects

Size
Body length: 1.2 to 1.4 inches (31 to 36 mm)

The scientific name for dragonflies and damselflies, Odonata, is derived from the Greek word *odon*, meaning "toothed." This refers to the spiny teeth that adult dragonflies use for chewing mosquitoes, gnats, midges, and other small flying insects. They locate their prey with the aid of two large compound eyes, each with between 10,000 and 30,000 individual lenses.

How to tell these insects apart
Dragonflies are generally larger and heavier than damselflies. Their eyes are so large they often meet at the top of the head. Damselfly eyes are bulging, yet never touching, giving their head a barbell shape. When dragonflies land, they always spread their wings apart. Damselflies generally hold their wings together above the body when at rest. The exception to this rule are the damselflies known as spreadwings, which keep their wings outspread when they are resting.

Ancient and agile flyers
The largest dragonfly wingspan known is 28 inches (71 cm), found in a fossil dating back nearly 250 million years. It is believed that the relatively high levels of oxygen in the air at the time allowed these ancient insects to grow so large. Today, the world's largest species is a

DISTRIBUTION

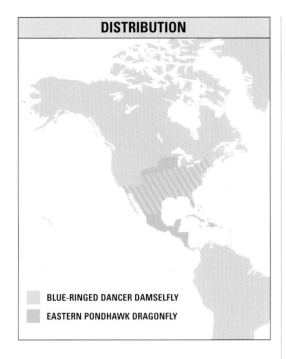

- ▨ BLUE-RINGED DANCER DAMSELFLY
- ▨ EASTERN PONDHAWK DRAGONFLY

Costa Rican damselfly with a 7.5-inch (19-cm) wingspan. The largest-known dragonfly living in the United States is the giant darner from the southwest states, which has a wingspan of more than 5.5 inches (14 cm).

Dragonflies have four long wings that are sometimes brightly colored. They are supported by a network of delicate veins. Powerful flight muscles can generate up to 40 wingbeats per second. In faster flight, the forewings and hind wings beat together, while slower flight is achieved by moving each pair of wings independently. Most of the lift required to fly is provided by the flapping of the wing, but some additional lift is provided by the veins; they cause tiny vortices (swirls of air) above the wing, which help the insect save energy as it flies. Some species can fly at speeds of up to 35 mph (56 km/h). They can hover with ease, and they can even fly backward for a short distance. In addition to wings, the adult thorax (midbody) has three pairs of legs.

The mating game

Males of the larger dragonfly species patrol territories along the water's edge, driving off potential rivals. Territories vary from 1 to 10 feet (0.3 to 3 m) in width, with larger species generally having larger territories. The length of the territory may reach 30 feet (9 m), limited only by the long-range vision of the male. As a female enters the area, the male approaches to mate.

The male reaches behind the head of the female with claspers at the tip of his abdomen and grasps her neck, in the case of damselflies, or head, in the case of dragonflies. Both sexes share the effort of flying, like two cyclists on a

KEY FACTS

Name
Eastern pondhawk dragonfly (*Erythemis simplicicollis*)

Distinctive features
Female and newly emerged male are green; mature male is blue

Habitat
Quiet, still water

Food
Adult eats small flying insects; nymph eats aquatic insects

Size
Body length: 1.7 inches (43 mm)

▼ *Dragonfly nymphs are fierce underwater predators, and, in addition to aquatic insects, can catch tadpoles and other small vertebrates.*

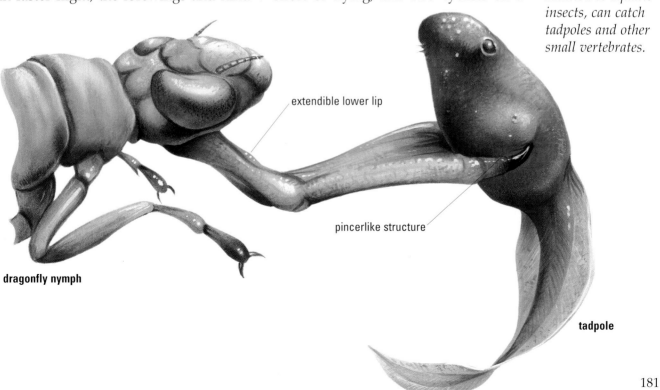

extendible lower lip

pincerlike structure

dragonfly nymph

tadpole

181

▲ *An adult hairy dragonfly slowly emerges from the skin of its nymph stage.*

Damselfly parasites

Damselflies are often infested with parasitic water mites. These tiny animals drink fluids from the bodies of their hosts. In low numbers they have little effect, but damselflies with large infestations die more quickly and lay fewer eggs.

The mites can also have an effect on the ability of a damselfly to reproduce. They can cause asymmetry in males (one side of the body appears slightly different from the other). Asymmetrical males are less likely to attract females and are therefore less likely to reproduce. A preference for symmetry is seen in many animals, including humans.

Some female dragonflies insert their eggs into the tissues of aquatic plants. Others bury them in mud or sand, or release them directly into the water. Eggs are laid singly or in small groups to ensure that the nymphs (young forms) will not have to compete with each other for food.

Laying eggs under water

Some male damselflies stay with the females through the egg-laying process. Females lay their eggs inside the tissues of submerged plants. They accomplish this task by completely submerging themselves under water, while the still-attached male remains above water. The surface tension of the water makes this a tricky business for the female. Afterward, the male may fly upward to help pull her back to the surface.

The length of time from egg to adult varies from species to species. Some mature in less than a month, but others take five or six years. Most species spend most of their lives under water as nymphs. However, the nymphs of some tropical species inhabit the moist leaf litter on the forest floor. Still others live in small isolated pockets of water found in the leaves of plants that cover the branches and trunks of rain forest trees high above the ground. Some North American dragonfly larvae construct tunnels in muddy bogs, emerging at night to hunt for insects and spiders.

bike. While still in midair, the female dragonfly curves her long, thin abdomen down and forward. Eventually, it comes into contact with the reproductive organs of the male.

Like the adults, young dragonflies are fierce predators. Their elongated lower lip is hinged at its base and can be extended like an extra arm. At the end of the lip are two jawlike structures armed with sharp teeth. This lip is thrust forward with tremendous speed to seize insects, worms, and occasionally small fish and other vertebrates such as tadpoles. The prey can be up to 1 inch (2.5 cm) away. When not in use, the lip is folded underneath the body.

Jet propulsion

Nymphs absorb oxygen directly from the water. Damselfly nymphs have three leaflike gills attached to the tip of the abdomen. The gills of dragonfly nymphs are located in the walls at the end of the digestive system. Water is alternately drawn in and forced out of the end of the abdomen. Not only does this allow the nymphs to breathe, but it also lets them jet-propel themselves quickly through the water.

When the nymphs are ready to become adults, they leave the water at night to crawl up onto plants or rocks to

molt. The skin of the nymph splits to reveal the body of the new adult. With their soft, pale bodies, the emerging adults are vulnerable to attack by birds or other predators. The insects wait for their wing membranes to harden before taking to the wing.

The legs of adult dragonflies are rarely used for walking. Instead, they form a basket for scooping up small flies and other prey while on the wing. Dragonflies can capture and eat up to 300 mosquitoes in one day.

Conservation

The most significant threat to dragonflies is the loss of their aquatic habitats. Only by protecting the bogs, ponds, streams, and rivers in which they breed and develop can populations of these insects be conserved. Many species of dragonflies and damselflies are endangered, including the Florida spiketail dragonfly, which is limited to two small populations in Florida. Hawaii is home to 22 species of *Megalagrion* damselflies, all of which are endangered. Perhaps the rarest North American dragonfly is Hine's emerald dragonfly. The nymphs of this species live in shallow, slow-moving water at a couple of sites in Illinois and Michigan.

▲ *Many dragonflies are beautifully colored. These colors are used for display, either against rivals or to attract a mate.*

◀ *The head of a dragonfly. Each compound eye may have as many as 30,000 individual lenses.*

SEE ALSO

- *Alderfly*
- *Caddis fly*
- *Endangered species*
- *Insect evolution*
- *Mayfly*
- *Sponge fly*
- *Stone fly*

DUNG BEETLE

Both the adults and larvae of these scarab beetles feed on animal feces. They are important in many ecosystems around the world since they remove and recycle dung.

There are several groups of scarab beetles that feed on feces. Together, these groups are collectively called the dung beetles. There are around 8,000 species of dung beetles known, and they live all around the world, except for a few islands and the cold polar regions.

Species living in the tropics tend to be larger than those living in cooler areas to the north and south. Most dung beetles are strong fliers, with sensitive antennae. They search for food either while flying or while perching on leaves. The last three segments of a dung beetle's antennae can be spread apart to expose the sensitive inner surface to passing chemicals in the air.

Burrowers and ball rollers
After detecting the odor of the feces, a pair of beetles will fly down and begin to break off small pieces. The beetles have to work quickly before flies have a chance to lay their eggs on the dung.

▼ *Dung beetles on elephant droppings in Zimbabwe. These beetles are most common in areas with many large mammals.*

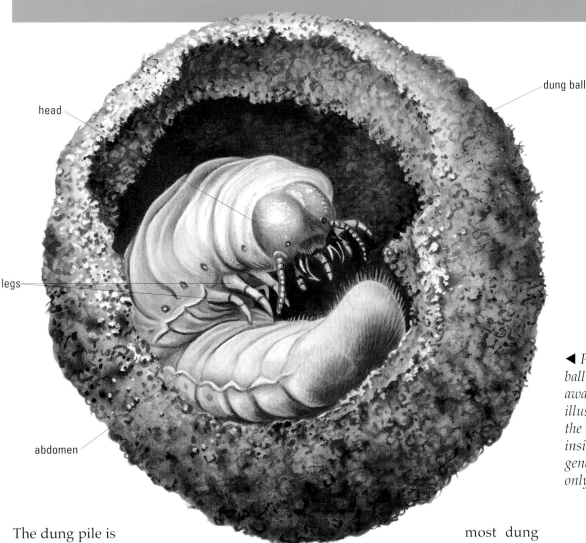

head

dung ball

legs

abdomen

◀ *Part of a dung ball has been cut away in this illustration to show the beetle larva inside. Dung balls generally contain only one larva.*

The dung pile is generally too large to be defended by a single pair of beetles, so the beetles have to move manageable amounts of it elsewhere. Some species pack pieces of the dung into a tunnel dug nearby or under the main pile of dung. These beetles are referred to as burrowers.

Other species form the dung into a ball and roll it away, before burying it in a more distant tunnel. These are called ball rollers. Often, there is competition as newly arrived pairs of beetles try to steal the ball of dung.

Egg laying

Once the food is buried, the female beetle lays eggs either directly on the food or in a chamber located nearby. The larvae are fat white grubs that feed inside the dung supplied to them by their parents. There is usually only one larva in each ball or piece of dung. In most dung beetles, the adults do not care for the larvae, but in a few species, the female stays until they have completed their development.

Not all dung beetles go to the trouble of finding and burying their own food. Some sneak into the burrows of other, usually larger, dung beetles and lay their eggs on the food intended for the larvae of the other species.

Ways to feed on dung

Ball-rollers live mainly in warmer areas and include the common and familiar tumblebugs of the American West and Midwest. Adults of ball-rolling species have unusually long and curved hind legs, which they use to roll the dung balls. Burrowers, on the other hand, have short, stocky legs that they use to dig burrows, and front legs with large serrations (teeth) that they use to cut out and pack the small pieces of dung into

KEY FACTS

Name
Sacred scarab
(*Scarabeus sacer*)

Distinctive features
Large, black, and flattened; ends of middle and hind legs expanded into bladelike shapes; four teeth along edge of forelegs

Food
Adult and larva feed on dung

Behavior
Adult makes 2-inch (5-cm) dung ball using front legs; it rolls the dung with its hind legs

Breeding
Eggs laid in buried dung ball

Size
1 to 1.5 inches (25 to 38 mm) long

DISTRIBUTION

SACRED SCARAB

▶ *This pair of African dung beetles from Zambia are rolling a ball of dung away from the main pile.*

SEE ALSO

- *Beetle*
- *Carrion beetle*
- *Ground beetle*
- *Larva, nymph, and pupa*
- *Scarab beetle*

their tunnels. Since they spend much of their time underground, burrowers are not commonly seen by people and are not as well known as the ball-rolling dung beetles.

Dung beetles can be choosy

Adult dung beetles search for food both in the daytime and at night, and many species live only in certain kinds of habitats or on only a few kinds of dung. There are species that feed on only the dung of howler monkeys; another feeds solely on sloth dung. There are even some rare species that feed only on millipede or snail droppings. Dung beetles are most numerous in areas where there are lots of large mammals, such as the grasslands of Africa and the tropical rain forests of Central and South America. Studies of dung beetle populations can be used to predict the numbers of mammal species in an area, helping in the creation of many conservation areas and parks.

A much-revered beetle

Some large African dung beetles, known as sacred scarabs, played an important role in ancient Egyptian religion many thousands of years ago. The Sun god, Ra, was represented by the scarab, and the Sun was represented by the dung ball. The ball-rolling behavior symbolized Ra pushing the Sun across the sky.

In more recent times, some people believed that the sacred scarabs had supernatural powers and could ensure life after death. Amulets resembling beetles were often placed in tombs. Even today, many pieces of jewelry are scarab-shaped in the hope that they will bring good luck and a long life.

Dung beetles are important for ecosystems since they recycle and remove feces. In doing so, they keep pastures free of flies and parasites.

EARWIG

Earwigs are common and familiar insects. Active at night, they hide away under stones and logs during the day. Earwigs are very unusual insects because they care for their young.

The name *earwig* is derived from the superstition that these insects crawl into the ears of sleeping people. Since they like to hide in small, dark places, it is not unlikely that earwigs have occasionally taken refuge inside a warm and dark ear, but no more so than other insects seeking somewhere safe to hide.

About 1,350 species of earwigs are known worldwide, with most found in the tropics. Like cockroaches, several species have been transported around the world by shipping and trade. Earwigs are scavengers or predators, with most feeding on living or dead insects and plants. There are even a few parasitic species that live on the bodies of other animals. Earwigs are active at night, hiding by day under stones, logs, and bark. Others conceal themselves inside cracks in the soil or deep inside flowers. Some species prefer to live in caves or burrow through the soil. Earwigs are often social animals, living in groups of dozens or hundreds of individuals.

Earwig body form

Earwigs are long, flattened insects that come in various shades of brown or black. The head projects forward and is equipped with chewing mouthparts. The first pair of wings has evolved into tough, leathery elytra (wing cases). These protect the delicate second pair of wings, which are used for flying. Some species lack wings altogether and are flightless. Earwigs sometimes fly on bright sunny days or toward lights at night. The long flexible abdomen ends in a pair of strong movable forceps, called cerci. The cerci of the adult male are larger and more pincerlike than those of the female or the nymph (young form). Both males

◀ *A European earwig foraging for food. These adaptable insects hunt other insects, and also feed on a range of dead animal and plant material.*

KEY FACTS

Name
European earwig (*Forficula auricularia*)

Distinctive features
Golden brown body; pincerlike forceps at tip of abdomen

Behavior
Nocturnal; hides under stones and logs by day

Breeding
Female cares for eggs and nymphs

Food
Insects; decaying animal and plant material

Size
0.5 to 0.75 inches (12 to 19 mm) long

▼ *The male European earwig has longer cerci than the female.*

DISTRIBUTION

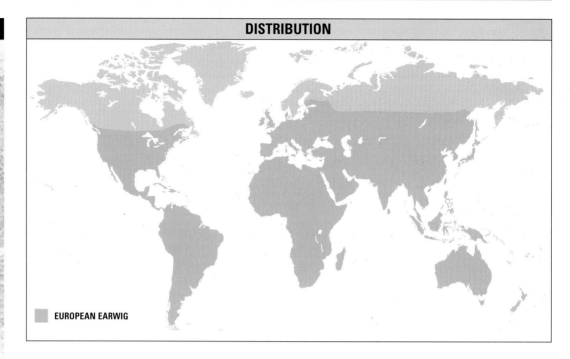

EUROPEAN EARWIG

and females use their cerci for defense, capturing prey, and folding and unfolding the wings. Males also use them to battle with rivals. Despite the presence of this fierce-looking weapon, earwigs are completely harmless to humans.

Twenty-two species of earwigs are known in North America, ranging in size from 0.4 to 1.2 inches (10 to 30 mm) in length. Many of these earwigs have been introduced from Europe and the tropics. The European earwig is dark brown with a distinctly reddish head and wing covers and pale legs and antennae. It is between 0.5 and 0.75 inches (12 and 19 mm) long, and it lives throughout the United States and areas of southern Canada, as well as most other parts of the globe.

The riparian earwig is a tropical species common throughout the southern United States. Its body is pale brown or chestnut, with very distinct black markings, and is about 1 inch (25 mm) long. The adult ring-legged earwig is wingless and has a dark brown body with pale yellow legs marked with rings. This earwig is around 0.5 inches (12 mm) in length and is found in southern Canada and the southern United States, where it is most common along the coast.

Earwig food

Some species eat plants such as mosses. Others devour flower petals and pollen, causing damage to ornamental and garden crops. Earwigs are also known to invade beehives and eat honey. As predators and scavengers, earwigs consume insects, spiders, and mites, dead or alive. Ring-legged earwigs damage stored plant and meat products and can become pests. A few Asian and African earwigs are parasitic. These insects live most of their lives on the

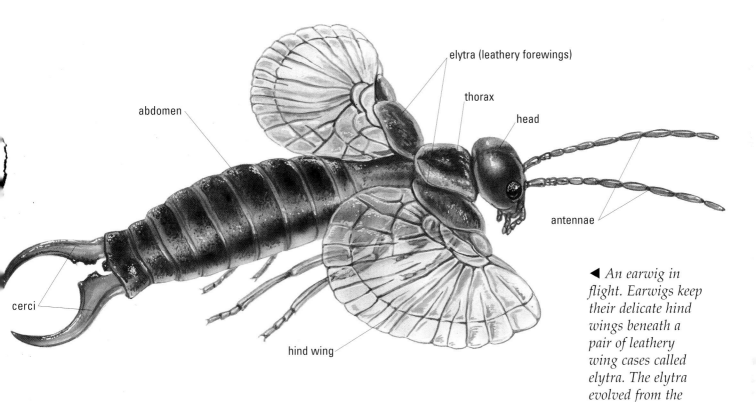

elytra (leathery forewings)

thorax

head

abdomen

antennae

cerci

hind wing

◀ *An earwig in flight. Earwigs keep their delicate hind wings beneath a pair of leathery wing cases called elytra. The elytra evolved from the forewings.*

bodies of free-tailed bats and giant pouched rats. They feed on skin and hair, and they have claws to help them hold on. Unlike other earwigs, these parasitic species do not lay eggs but give birth to live young.

Caring for their young

After laying eggs, most insects leave their young to survive alone. Some earwigs are different, and guard and care for their eggs and newly hatched nymphs. The female first digs a

◀ *A female earwig guards her eggs, some of which have already hatched. The eggs are laid into a chamber that she has excavated underneath a stone or log.*

chamber in the soil or leaf litter. She then lays smooth oval eggs that are pearly white, yellowish, or cream. The female frequently turns the eggs, and she keeps them moist and free of fungi. The eggs hatch in as little as eight days in warmer climates, but they take a little longer under cooler conditions.

The nymphs remain in the chamber and are fed regurgitated (partly digested) food by the female. These young earwigs have straight, segmented cerci, and they undergo between four and six molts before reaching maturity. One or two generations are born each year.

Defense against predators

Ants, predatory beetles, centipedes, and spiders feed on earwigs, and some earwig species are parasitized by flies and roundworms. Earwigs use their powerful cerci to defend themselves. Some species have abdominal glands that release an unpleasant fluid when the earwig is disturbed. *Doru taeniatum* has yellow markings on its wing cases, which warn that predators may be in for a shock if they get too close. This earwig can aim its discharge very accurately

Strange cerci

The cerci, or forceps, of male European earwigs are much larger than those of the females and nymphs. They are used by the males for fighting with rivals. Males fight for dominance over other males, since dominant males tend to produce more offspring.

Earwigs with large forceps are better at fighting than those with smaller ones. Recent research has shown, however, that male earwigs with large cerci do not always have young with large cerci. Instead, environmental factors influence the growth of the young earwigs and determine the size of their forceps. Even if the father of a batch of eggs had long forceps, some of the young will still have shorter ones. The main factor determining cerci length is probably the amount of food available to the mother during the time she provides regurgitated (part-digested) food for her young in the brood chamber.

by curling its abdomen. This allows the earwig to use its cerci in defense at the same time. The secretion from its abdomen contains acidic chemicals that deter most predators from attacking. These chemicals are stored as crystals in the glands; the openings to the glands are tiny, and this stops the crystals from squeezing through.

Earwigs as pests

Earwigs may be very abundant in some gardens, and they can cause damage to ornamental plants. The European earwig is very well known to gardeners, since it often feeds on garden plants.

The striped earwig prefers other food, such as flies, springtails, and other small insects, but it will feed on plants when animal food is scarce.

cerci

elytron

nymphs

regurgitated food

◄ *Some female earwigs feed their nymphs with regurgitated food. The mother vomits up this partly digested food from her stomach.*

GLOSSARY

abdomen: the rear body section of insects, spiders, and other arthropods

antennae (an-TEH-nee): sensitive jointed feelers on the heads of insects

arthropod (AHR-thruh-PAHD): animal with several pairs of jointed limbs and a hard outer covering (exoskeleton)

asymmetry (A-suh-MEH-tree): differences in shape between two sides of an animal's body

book lung: a series of leaflike plates through which scorpions and some spiders breathe

carrion: the rotting flesh of dead animals

cephalothorax (SEH-fuh-luh-THOR-AKS): the fused head and thorax of a spider

chelicerae (kih-LIH-suh-ree): appendages near an arachnid's mouth; those of spiders carry fangs

digestion: process of breaking down food into easily absorbed substances

elytra: wing cases of insects such as beetles that protect the hind wings

exoskeleton: the hard outer covering of an arthropod; contains chitin (KEYE-tuhn)

gall: bumps of tissue produced by plants in response to being attacked by certain insects

gill: breathing organ of water-living invertebrates and some land-living species, such as pill bugs; it draws in oxygen

halteres (HOL-TIRS): a pair of clublike organs used by flies to balance in flight

honeydew: sugary liquid released by many bugs and some caterpillars as a waste product after feeding on plant sap

host: animal that provides food and usually a place to live for a parasite

insecticide (in-SEHK-tuh-SEYED): a chemical that kills insects

larva (LAR-vuh): young form of insect that looks different from the adult, lives in a different habitat (type of place), and eats different foods

mimicry (MIH-mih-kree): when an animal uses color, sound, or behavior to disguise itself as something else

molt: shedding of the exoskeleton by an arthropod as it grows

neurotoxin (NOOR-oh-TAHK-suhn): poison that acts on the nervous system

nocturnal: active at night

nymph (NIHMF): young form of insect that looks similar to the adult and usually lives in a similar habitat (type of place)

omnivore (AHM-nih-VOR): animal that can feed on any type of organism

ootheca (OH-uh-THEE-kuh): case containing a number of eggs; produced by insects such as mantises and cockroaches

ovipositor (OH-vuh-PAH-zuh-tuhr): tube on a female insect's abdomen for laying eggs

oxygen: gas in the air or dissolved in water that all animals need to live

parasite: organism that feeds on another organism called a host; the host may be damaged but is not killed by the parasite

pheromone (FEH-ruh-MOHN): chemical released by an insect, often to attract mates or to direct other insects to food

pupa (PYOO-puh): stage during which a larva transforms into an adult insect

queen: egg-laying reproductive female in a colony of social insects, including bees, ants, wasps, and termites

scavenger: animal that feeds on the bodies of dead animals

serrations: toothlike projections from a limb or other appendage

sperm: male sex cell that fuses with a female egg to create a new individual

spiracle (SPIH-rih-kuhl): opening through which arthropods breathe

symbiosis (SIM-bee-OH-suhs): a biological relationship between two different species

thorax: midbody section of an insect to which legs and wings are attached

vector: animal that carries a disease-causing agent but is not usually affected by it

vertebrate (VUHR-tuh-bruht): animal with a backbone, such as a bird, reptile, or mammal

vortex: swirl of air created by the wings of flying animals, such as bats, birds, and insects

INDEX

Page numbers in **bold** refer to main articles; those in *italics* refer to picture captions.